Leonard Bacon

Christian Self-Culture

The origin and development of a Christian life

Leonard Bacon

Christian Self-Culture
The origin and development of a Christian life

ISBN/EAN: 9783337259938

Printed in Europe, USA, Canada, Australia, Japan

Cover: Foto ©Lupo / pixelio.de

More available books at **www.hansebooks.com**

OR THE ORIGIN AND DEVELOPMENT OF A CHRISTIAN LIFE.

BY

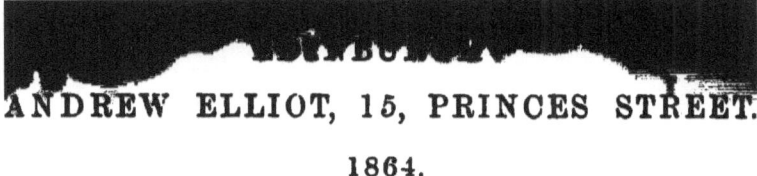

ANDREW ELLIOT, 15, PRINCES STREET.

1864.

PREFACE.

THE author of this book has had a long experience in the ministry of the gospel. As he looks back to the time when he entered on that ministry, and inquires of himself what progress he has made in the knowledge of the gospel, he finds that in nothing has the habit of his mind undergone a greater change, than in his sense of the freedom with which he may offer salvation to men in the name of Christ. Year after year, without becoming conscious of any deviation from those views of Christian doctrine which are commonly recognised as "evangelical," he has been acquiring a more enlarged and unembarrassed conception of the gospel, as opening a way in which any man who will can be saved. Surely, if there be any first principle in Christianity, which is to be held at all hazards, and which no theological system or theory may be permitted to darken, it is the principle that salvation from sin, and from the death which is the wages of sin, is offered, frankly and without equivocation, to all men.

This book, therefore, regards the beginning and progress of the Christian life from that point of view to which the author has been brought by his experience in the ministry of the gospel, as well as by his study of the Scriptures. It assumes that in the case of every reader, whoever he may be, the beginning of a new life is possible by the grace of God in Christ. It assumes that every man may avail himself of all those offers and promises which the gospel sets before him; may accept and appropriate the offered forgiveness of sins; may act on the assurance that God is willing to give the Holy Spirit in answer to prayer; may confidently trust in Christ's presence and friendship; may immediately undertake to follow Christ, striving to overcome his own selfish and unbelieving habits, and hoping to get the victory. Therefore, it offers to the reader, not a psychological explanation of the change which takes place in conversion, nor any metaphysical disquisition about the will, but only some practical counsels for the beginning and progress of a Christian life. If it is to do any good, it must be read, not for theological speculation and discussion, nor with the expectation that it will produce its effect by some impression on the feelings, but for the practical purpose of Christian self-culture.

It should not be forgotten that in this book the Christian life is considered only in one aspect. The Christian life is the life of one who, at the call of God, under the mediation and leadership of Christ, and in reliance on the promise of the Holy Spirit, has undertaken to be a new creature in Christ, to be progressively transformed by the renewing of his mind, to train himself in and for the service of God, and so to make the most of himself as a living soul whose chief end is to glorify God and enjoy him for ever. Considered in this aspect, it is Christian self-culture. Considered in another aspect, it is Christian experience ; and in that aspect it has often been described and analysed, with careful discrimination between the genuine and the false. Let not this book, because it treats only of Christian self-culture, be considered as denying or doubting the reality of Christian experience. Christian self-culture, earnestly undertaken in reliance on the grace of God, and diligently pursued, will involve in its progress all that is essential to a full experience of the gospel as a quickening and transforming power.

With these explanations the author sends forth his work upon its errand, praying, and asking the prayers of others, that God's blessing may attend the reading of it.

CHAPTER I.

THE BEGINNING.

THE DESIGN OF THIS BOOK. WHAT ARE YOU IN YOUR OWN CON-
SCIOUSNESS?—YOU ARE A LIVING SOUL; YOUR DESTINY CANNOT
BE COMPLETED IN THIS LIFE; YOUR FACULTIES ARE PROOF THAT
YOU WERE MADE FOR A FREE AND INTELLIGENT SERVICE OF GOD;
YOU ARE CAPABLE OF UNLIMITED PROGRESS. CONNEXION BETWEEN
THE PRESENT AND THE FUTURE:—NOW OR NEVER YOU MUST BE
TRAINED FOR YOUR HEREAFTER. DIFFICULTIES AND DISADVAN-
TAGES:—POWER OF SIN. ENCOURAGEMENT:—OFFERS AND HOPES
PRESENTED IN THE GOSPEL. NATURE OF THE CHRISTIAN SELF-DIS-
CIPLINE:—IT IS A DISCIPLINE IN DUTY, AIDED BY THE MEANS OF
GRACE.

A

"Come unto me, all ye that labour and are heavy laden, and I will give you rest. Take my yoke upon you, and learn of me ; for I am meek and lowly in heart : and ye shall find rest unto your souls. For my yoke is easy, and my burden is light."—MATT. XI. 28-30.

"Behold, now is the accepted time ; behold, now is the day of salvation."—2 COR. VI. 2.

"It is appointed unto men once to die, but after this the judgment."—HEB. IX. 27.

"Whatsoever a man soweth, that shall he also reap. For he that soweth to his flesh, shall of the flesh reap corruption ; but he that soweth to the Spirit, shall of the Spirit reap life everlasting." GAL. VI. 7, 8.

"Know ye not that they which run in a race run all, but one receiveth the prize ? So run, that ye may obtain. And every man that striveth for the mastery is temperate in all things. Now they do it to obtain a corruptible crown, but we an incorruptible. I therefore so run, not as uncertainly ; so fight I, not as one that beateth the air."—1 COR. IX. 24-26.

"Exercise thyself unto godliness."—1 TIM. IV. 7.

"I can do all things through Christ which strengtheneth me." PHIL. IV. 13.

The Beginning.

TRULY religious life is often represented in the Scriptures as a life of self-discipline and self-culture. Viewed in this aspect, a really Christian life is the life of one who, under the influence of Christian views and motives, and in the use of those means and helps which God has given him in giving him the gospel, is striving to make the most of himself for the ends for which he was created, and to bring himself into the highest possible conformity to the will and the image of God. Thus the apostle Paul describes the Christian life, and particularly his own life as a Christian man, in words and images borrowed from the discipline by which the candidates for prizes in the athletic games of Greece were exercised and trained to their utmost capability of bodily activity and power. Thus, too, he charges his friend and former pupil, Timothy, "Exercise thyself unto godliness." In other words : Train thyself, by a religious discipline, to the knowledge and service of God. A man who has set his heart upon winning the prize in the Olympian or the Isthmian games, trains himself to that end ; he

goes daily into the gymnasium, to leap, to run, to wrestle, to develop and cultivate the power of his muscles by every sort of practice : so " exercise thyself unto godliness."

Reader, this book is designed to help you in beginning and pursuing a Christian life. It is designed to help you by persuasion and by friendly counsel. The religion which it commends to you is not merely the intellectual reception of a certain doctrinal scheme ; nor is it merely an experience of excited feeling ; it is a life, a thoughtful and earnest way of living, a life of self-discipline. A religious life is not a life of forms, or of outward proprieties and moralities ; it is the interior life of a soul training itself and developing its own nature aright,—a soul humbly, yet with resolute diligence, educating its own moral and spiritual faculties into conformity with truth and with God. Think, as you read, that a friend is speaking to you. I wish to bring home to your thoughts the reasonableness, the duty, the necessity of such a life. I am to make you understand, if I can, what is a truly religious life, and what it is to be a religious man, religion being viewed under the form of Christian self-culture. Allow me thus to help you, if I can, in beginning such a life. And may God help me while I write, and help you when you read.

We begin, then, with this question : *Have you ever considered what you are ?* In order to any right understanding of the subject, or any conscious interest in it, you must be willing to think, and to turn your thought upon yourself. You must reflect ; for serious thought turned inward is reflection. You must reflect on the nature, the capabilities, and the future of your own existence ; on your faculties of thought and will, and your capacity of progress ; on the career for which you were created, and to which your powers and capabilities, as a living soul, are adapted.

What are you ? Are you an animal merely, with some few faculties that give you the advantage over other animals ; while they, in their turn, have in some other respects the advantage over you ? If so, eat and drink, for to-morrow you die. But you start back from such a conclusion ; you know that you differ from the noblest of brutes, not in degree, not by those incidents and circumstances merely that constitute variety, but in kind. These limbs and organs of yours, this material body and its parts and members, are yours, indeed ; but they are not yourself. You are, in your own consciousness, a living spirit, reasonable, voluntary, determining your own course and character. Inferior creatures are bound by laws which they know not, and cannot resist ; but you are bound by laws which speak through your reason to your voluntary nature, and which you resist or obey at your option. You can perceive and grasp truth ; not merely the phenomena that strike your senses as they strike the senses of inferior creatures,—but truth. You can perceive not merely colours, forms, and distances, as inferior creatures see them, but beauty and grandeur spread like a veil of light over all the creation of God. You can perceive not merely pleasure and pain, consequent in various degrees on various acts ; but obligation, duty, the right and the wrong, with the beauty of the one and the hatefulness of the other. Your human body—the frail thing that eats, drinks, sleeps, is weary and sick, decays and is resolved into dust—how small a part is it of yourself! *You*, in your consciousness and personality, are something else than the organization through which you are in communication with material nature. Your *being* is that which thinks, reasons, knows, inquires, believes, remembers, imagines, loves, hates, hopes, fears, determines, reflects, approves, condemns, rejoices, repents. You are a living spirit, created in the likeness of God, created for freedom and responsibility. Have you ever considered, thoughtfully, what you are?

Think again. Can such an existence as yours accomplish all its destiny in this short course of mortal life ? You were created for more than this. There was an hour when you began to be ; but when will you cease to be ? Death, indeed, is at hand ; there will soon be a great change in your condition, and none can adequately tell you what that change will be ; but the instinct of immortality within you constrains you to look forth into the infinite future with expectation that will not be suppressed. This mortal life, under this material organization, is only the beginning of your history, a history that will have no end. Have you ever thought of this ?

Think of it now.   Think what it is to be a living soul, rational, responsible, immortal.   •

Let your soul thus rouse itself from its unreflective habit to the consciousness of what you are, and another view will open to your thoughts.   For what were you made with these capabilities and faculties ?   The world is full of life, and full of the manifested power and skill and love of its Creator ; but, of all the living creatures that you see, you only, and your fellow-men, are capable of knowing God.   Other creatures do his will ignorantly and involuntarily ; you are capable of rendering to him, or of withholding from him, an intelligent and willing service. This, then, is what you were made for,—to know God, to behold with adoring acknowledgment his manifestations of himself, to commune with him in thought and action, to be his willing servant and his loving child, and to be blessed in his service and his love.   If you were made for this, as your consciousness assures you that you were, then to this you must be trained, to this your character must be formed, or you miss the " end and aim " for which you came into existence.

Think also (for just here it is natural for you to think of it) what your progress may be in the future.   Take away the limits which are inseparable from the present condition of the soul, bounded on every side by the grossness and the frailty of this material organization, and what limit can be set to the progress which you shall hereafter make in knowledge, in the intensity of love or hate, and in the capacity of blessedness or wretchedness ?   With what a treasure, then, are you embarked upon the sea of existence ; and how important is it that your soul be so trained and disciplined as to secure this infinite treasure !

Having led you to these reflections on your own nature, with its marvellous powers and capabilities, I now propose another question : *Have you ever considered, with due thoughtfulness, what connexion there may be between your present life and your life hereafter ?* Think how far your soul's well-being after death may be dependent on what your soul shall have become before death.

I am not asking you to occupy your mind with useless conjectures, or with inferences from doubtful speculations. We have a sure word of prophecy.   God has given us intelligible certainties.   Now is the accepted time. After death is the judgment.   Every one shall receive according to that he hath done in the body.   You are now sowing that of which you will reap the infinite harvest hereafter ; and what a man soweth that shall he also reap ;   he that soweth to the flesh shall of the flesh reap corruption, and he that soweth to the Spirit shall of the Spirit reap life everlasting.   This life is your probation.   All is involved in the result of it. The character which your soul shall bear in the sight of God, at your departure from this mortal life, will determine your course and destiny in the immortal life to come.   Now or never your soul must be formed, by fit culture, for the love and service of God, as its chief end

and its immortal blessedness. Let this opportunity be
wasted, let your soul pass through this period of probation uneducated, undisciplined in God's service, unfitted
for that high career to which its faculties and its capacities
were destined, and when, in all the cycles of eternity,
will you find one opportunity to repair the infinite waste ?

And here another question presents itself : *Have you
ever considered how much has been already lost, and
under what difficulties and disadvantages the training
of your soul, for its immortal life of duty and of
blessedness, must be begun ?* The fact of your apostasy
from God, and of the effects which sin has already produced upon your spiritual nature, is a most material
fact in the problem of that moral and spiritual self-
culture to which you are invited.

In the education of your soul for the immortal love
and service of God, you have not only everything to
learn, but everything to unlearn. You must cease to
do evil, or you cannot learn to do well ; and this necessity of ceasing to do evil is what makes the task of
learning to do well so difficult. You are under the
power of habits, long-established and confirmed, which
it must be the first effort of a religious self-discipline to
break up and dislodge. From your earliest remem-
brance of yourself you have been governed, consciously
or unconsciously, by propensities which must be resisted
and subdued. This is not a trivial accident which has
befallen you, and which the better forces of your nature
must be expected to throw off by their spontaneous

working. You know there is nothing trivial or transient in the corruption which has taken hold of your spiritual nature, and has degraded you so far below what you ought to be, and so far below what you must yet become, unless your soul is wrecked for ever. Our present purpose does not require us to enter into any speculative explanations of the fact ; the fact itself is what concerns us now. The self-discipline to which you are invited is not merely to train the powers, and to unfold and direct the pure susceptibilities of an unfallen spirit ;—it is a remedial discipline, dealing with an apostate soul. It is a discipline designed and conducted for the recovery of a sinful soul ; aiming to humble it, to renew it, to purify it, to set it free from its bondage, to transform it into the resemblance of God's holiness, and thus to make it fit for the inheritance of the saints in light. Or rather, it is the life-long labour of such a soul, led by the grace of God to struggle for its own deliverance, to work out its own salvation with fear and trembling, to purify itself by obeying the truth through the Spirit, to exercise itself unto godliness. How important is it then to you, that this remedial discipline be undertaken without delay, and be maintained with ceaseless diligence to the end !

Here the question comes : *Is there any possibility, any reasonable hope of success in such an attempt ?* In answer to this question, I commend to your attention and your confidence the grace of God that is offered in the gospel.

The gospel of Christ does not merely propose the reward of eternal blessedness to those who are worthy of such an inheritance ; its grace is far ampler and richer than that. Read what the Saviour says : "If ye continue in my words, then are ye my disciples indeed, and ye shall know the truth, and the truth shall make you free." Hear him inviting you : "Come to me, all ye that labour and are heavy laden ; take my yoke upon you, and learn of me." The gospel is rich with promises like these, by which we may escape the corruption that is in the world, and may be made partakers of the divine nature (2 Pet. i. 4). It reveals not only heaven for the holy, but also (what is much more pertinent to our case) pardon for the guilty. It reveals not only God the Judge of all, but also Jesus the Mediator of the new covenant. Nor is this all, for, with the atoning Saviour, it also reveals and offers a renewing Spirit. To the believer in Christ, not only is there no more condemnation (Rom. viii. 1), but old things are passed away and all things are become new (2 Cor. vi. 17) ; and notwithstanding that corruption of his nature which sin has caused, he may learn to say with humble assurance, "I can do all things through Christ which strengtheneth me."

To you, then, the assurance is offered, that if you will come to God in Christ for pardon and grace ; if you will come, humbling yourself and repenting and asking for the Holy Spirit, you may undertake this course of self-discipline for immortal holiness with a

confident hope of success.   The gospel, with all its
grace, is set before you expressly for this end, that you
may be persuaded and enabled and encouraged to exercise yourself now in the service of God, and so to train
yourself for that higher and perfect service of God, which
will employ for ever the perfected spirits of the just.

I will now presume that you are ready to ask for
yourself, *What is the self-discipline to which I am invited ?*   What are the processes and methods, what the
means and helps, of this spiritual self-training ?

Understand, then, that the discipline to which you
are summoned is the discipline of duty, of voluntary
subjection to truth, of holiness, of the service of God.
Just that service of God to which you are called in this
world, whatever your particular field of service may be,
as determined by your place and your relations in society ;
that service, whatever it may be, which the providence
of God allots to you,—a service which you are to perform in the face of innumerable temptations, and which
involves a perpetual conflict with whatever is perverse
in your own habits and inclinations ; that service of
God, in your place and calling, is itself the most material part of the discipline by which you are to be trained
for a higher ministry hereafter.   By all those daily duties,
then, and all those daily cares, in which God would have
you serve Him and your fellow-men, you are to be trained
and exercised unto godliness.   He who, whether he eats
or drinks, or whatever he does, strives to do all to the
glory of God ; he who, in any sphere of toil, from the

loftiest to the lowliest, learns to do all things heartily to the Lord and not to men, is training himself effectually for immortal virtue.

Subsidiary to this discipline of daily duty, there are the various *means of grace*,—the means by which the soul is led and assisted in the performance of duty and in the culture of holy affections and habits. You know what these means of grace are. There is prayer, by which the soul comes into immediate communion with God, and receives immediately from him a quickening influence. By prayer you can exercise yourself to godliness. There is the religious duty of reflection in order to self-knowledge ; the devotional exercise of communing with your own heart, and inquiring into your own habits and condition before God, so that by growing more and more acquainted with yourself, you may grow in humility and penitence. In this way, you are to exercise yourself to godliness. There is also the exercise of an habitual watchfulness against temptation,—the habit of observing one's own weaknesses and spiritual dangers, and of keeping guard against them. By this you are to discipline and train your soul till you are always on your guard, incapable of a surprise. Need I insist on the right use of times and seasons, and of all special opportunities for cultivating those affections in which the soul has fellowship with God ? Whenever anything occurs that quickens your religious sensibilities—anything that brings God, eternity, heaven, near to your thoughts and feelings,—then is a time in which, if you will use the opportunity aright, you may effectually discipline your soul to godliness. And with all these, yet distinct from them all, there is that special intercourse with God which you may have in the devout and teachable study of his Word ; there is the house of God ; there is the fellowship of those who love God, and who walk by faith. In the use of all these *means of grace,* you are to train yourself to the blessedness of serving God in love for ever.

Such is the discipline of your own spiritual faculties and capabilities to which religion calls you. Such are the modes and processes by which you are to exercise yourself to godliness. Think now what sort of a discipline this is. Is it anything servile ? Is there any degradation in being subject to it ? Is there anything in it that you need be afraid of it ? Is it anything else than the highest and noblest culture of your spiritual and immortal nature ? To be without such discipline, to be left under the power of the habits and tendencies which this discipline proposes to resist and overcome, *that* is bondage, that is degradation, that is the soul's wretchedness and ruin. The great author and finisher of this discipline, the Divine Revealer of its promises and hopes, will make you free. " Come unto me," he says, " all ye that labour and are heavy laden, and I will give you rest. Take my yoke upon you, and learn of me : for I am meek and lowly in heart ; and ye shall find rest to your souls. For my yoke is easy, and my burden is light."

Reader ! have you entered upon this course of self-discipline, under the guidance of Christ ? Have you, reflecting on the nature, the capacities, and the destiny of your own soul, realizing the relations which connect this transient life with the infinite hereafter, remembering the fact of your apostasy and alienation from God, and trusting in the offered grace of the Gospel,—begun with earnest and resolute purpose to exercise yourself to godliness ? Are you daily practising this self-discipline, watchfully, diligently, and in the believing spirit of dependence on Christ ?

If you have not yet begun, begin to-day.

CHAPTER II.

WHEN TO BEGIN.

A COMMON EXCUSE. MISTAKES ABOUT CONVERSION. THE MISTAKE OF THINKING THAT YOU MUST MAKE SOME PREPARATION. THE MISTAKE OF THINKING THAT YOU MUST NOT TRUST IN CHRIST TILL YOU FEEL YOU HAVE BEEN CONVERTED. THE MISTAKE OF THINKING THAT AFTER CONVERSION EVERYTHING WILL BE EASY. HOW THE CHRISTIAN LIFE REALLY BEGINS. WILL YOU MAKE THIS BEGINNING NOW?

"Except a man be born again, he cannot see the kingdom of God."—JOHN III. 3.

"Murmur not among yourselves. No man can come to me, except the Father, who hath sent me, draw him. . . . Every man therefore that hath heard, and hath learned of the Father, cometh unto me."—JOHN VI. 43-45.

"If any man be in Christ, he is a new creature."—2 COR. V. 17.

"This is a faithful saying, and worthy of all acceptation, that Christ Jesus came into the world to save sinners."—1 TIM. I. 15.

"The grace of God that bringeth salvation hath appeared to all men, teaching us, that, denying ungodliness and worldly lusts, we should live soberly, righteously, and godly, in this present world; looking for that blessed hope, and the glorious appearing of the great God and our Saviour Jesus Christ; who gave himself for us, that he might redeem us from all iniquity, and purify unto himself a peculiar people, zealous of good works."—TIT. II. 11-14.

"Having therefore these promises, let us cleanse ourselves from all filthiness of the flesh and spirit, perfecting holiness in the fear of God."—2 COR. VII. 1.

When to Begin.

IT has been shown that the Gospel invites you to a life of moral and spiritual self-discipline in preparation for the life to come. But you perhaps excuse yourself by saying that a Christian life must begin with being born again. You tell me, perhaps, that all counsels and persuasions in reference to a Christian life are properly addressed to the converted, and that you, inasmuch as you have had no experience of the great change in which a Christian life begins, have no present concern in the subject which I am commending to your attention.

Let us then look this difficulty fairly in the face, and see what becomes of your excuse. I would by no means intimate that there is no difficulty in your way, nor that your conversion from a thoughtless and selfish life to a life of humble and earnest preparation for eternity is dependent simply on your sovereign volition. I would by no means lessen your sense of your dependence on God for those merciful influences of his under which so great a change in you must be effected. But may it not be that you have taken up some erroneous conception of what that change is which the Scriptures call being born again ?   May it not be that if you will deliberately and fairly reconsider what the gospel requires of you and what it offers you, and will cease to resist the influences which at this moment are working within you and moving you to a decision, you will see and feel the fallacy of your excuse ?   It may help you to understand yourself and the nature and extent of your responsibility for your own wellbeing, if I succeed in explaining to you some of the common mistakes about conversion.   Let us inquire a little into your theory about the beginning of a Christian life.

Perhaps you have fallen into the habit of supposing that your conversion to Christ and your privilege of appropriating as your own the offers and promises which are set before you in his name, must be the result of some preparatory work on your part.   I shall not argue with you on this point.   What more need I say than that such a habit of mind contradicts and excludes the first right conception of the gospel ?   Why do you need Christ ?   Your need is that without him you are helpless.   The simplest and most comprehensive statement of the gospel is that " Christ Jesus came into the world to save sinners."   If you were now just what Saul of Tarsus was when he was on his way from Jerusalem to Damascus, the first thing for you to do, at the moment of coming to yourself, would be, not a preparation for conversion, but conversion itself, not a getting yourself ready for coming to Christ, but an actual turning to Christ, with that question of a submissive and confiding soul, "Lord, what wilt thou have me to do?" If you were at this hour the guiltiest of men in the sight of God, the first thing for you to do would be, not to establish a new character as a preparation for trusting in Christ, but to trust in Christ in order to your becoming a new creature. Remember what the true idea of the gospel is. It is God's way of saving men from their sins. It is God's revealed method of turning men to himself, and of training them in this world for immortal activity and blessedness in the world to come.

Just here another mistake sometimes occurs to hinder the beginning of the Christian life. Perhaps you are in the habit of thinking that the consciousness of a great change wrought within you by the power of God must precede your act of trusting in Christ. Some such theory of conversion is sometimes deduced, indistinctly, or even unconsciously, from the necessity of being born again. The promises and hopes of the gospel, it is said, are only for those who have been born again, and not for the unregenerate or unconverted. "The work of saving me from my sins," it is said, "is God's work and not mine; how then am I to begin unless I am first assured that God has begun his saving work within me; how can I claim and appropriate the Christian hope of emancipation from sin, and of victory over it; how can I enter upon the Christian life of self-discipline for immortal holiness, unless I am conscious in some way that God has called me, and that I am born again ? "

The answer to all this is that you are mistaken in your theory of how God works in renewing and saving men.   If you will suffer yourself to be taught by the Holy Scriptures, you will find that they give no support to such a theory.   Where or how do the Scriptures teach that you must be born again *before* you accept the pardon and the grace which God is offering you ? They teach you, indeed, that " if any man be in Christ he is a new creature ;" but they do not teach that any man becomes a new creature while he is out of Christ, still less that his being in Christ is because he became a new creature while he was yet out of Christ.   They teach, indeed, that " except a man be born again, he cannot see the kingdom of God ;" but they do not teach that any man is born again, or can be, *before* he accepts the gospel as his hope, and trusts in Christ as the power that is to save him, still less that he must have the consciousness that he is born again before he can believe in the Saviour of sinners.   Christ, indeed, teaches you, " No man can come to me, except the Father, who hath sent me, draw him ;" but he does not teach you that the Father is not at this moment drawing you, nor that you must wait for any new consciousness before you accept the hopes and promises which the gospel offers.   On the contrary, the Scriptures are full of a very opposite sort of doctrine, inviting you and all men to be saved, warning you against the peril of neglecting so great salvation, and urging you to work out your salvation, for the reason that it is God, who is working in you to will and to do.

This error, in regard to the beginning of the Christian life, is closely related to another. Perhaps your theory supposes not only that the consciousness of a great change wrought within you by the power of God must go before, instead of following, your personal confidence in Christ as a Saviour for you, but also that the change which you are waiting for will take away the necessity of further effort and conflict in the Christian life. Perhaps the theory which you have indistinctly and unthinkingly adopted, concerning the work of God in drawing you to Christ and making you a new crea-ture, implies that, after you have once passed through that change, your progress in the new life will be, not by thoughtful and resolute diligence,—not by struggles against temptation and the force of old habits,—not by intelligent aspiration and strenuous endeavour,—but by mere propensity, like the propensity to selfishness and unbelief to which you have heretofore yielded the domi-nion over your soul. I apprehend that few mistakes in regard to the change at the beginning of a Christian life are more common than this among those who, having been taught in some form of sound words the great and true doctrine of regeneration and sanctification by the grace of God, have accepted that doctrine in a merely traditionary way, instead of deriving it directly from the Scriptures. They find that now they are worldly, selfish,

and thoughtless, without effort; that they are carried
along by mere propensity; that they are borne, as it
were, upon a mighty current; and they heedlessly presume that, if ever they are born again, the current will
be reversed, as in a change of tide; the propensity will
incline the other way, as the inclination of the scale-
beam changes with the shifting of the weights; and that
a life of faith and prayer and holy love will be as easy
as a worldly life now is.   Surely I need not remind any
thoughtful soul how contrary all this is to the whole
course of God's teaching in his recorded Word.   You
know well enough, if you will remember what you know,
that the beginning of a Christian life—the change which
takes place in conversion when God draws the soul to
Christ—the change which takes place when the man is
born again, and becomes a citizen in the kingdom of
God,—is not after such a fashion.   The being born again,
the coming to Christ, the conversion of the soul to God,
the becoming a new creature, the great transition from
death in trespasses and sins to a new and spiritual life,—
is the beginning of a life-long conflict with inward propensities, as well as with outward temptations.

Think, then, what that life is to which the gospel
invites you, and you will have a clearer knowledge of
what the beginning of that life must be.   All the words
and images by which the greatness of that change is
represented to you, or by which God's mercy in bringing
that change to pass is commended to your humble and
grateful adoration, will become alike intelligible and im-

pressive, when you remember distinctly what sort of a life it is to which the gospel calls you. Just remember that the gospel calls you to a life of humble, praying, and constant self-discipline, under the guidance of God's Word and with his promised help, preparing you for immortal well-doing and well-being in the life to come ; and you will hardly fail to see what the beginning of such a life must be. Remember that such a life must needs be a life of free obedience to the will of God, and of earnest self-denial for the sake of pleasing him ; a life of conflict with temptation, and of resolute watchfulness ; a life of trusting dependence on Christ, and of habitual looking for help in time of need ; a life of practical love to God, testified by the doing of his will, and of practical love to men, testified by doing good ; a life, therefore, of progress, by God's blessing on your diligence in the face of obstacles, and under the consciousness of infirmity. Can you not see, with the offers and promises of the gospel before you, what you are to do, and what is wanting in your case to the commencement of such a life ?

Just this is wanting in your case : not some preparation for beginning such a life, but simply a beginning ; not some preparation that shall make it possible for you to lay hold on the hope set before you, or that shall make it right for you to do so, but simply that you accept the mercy and help which God offers you. That new life to which Christ calls you begins with believing that he calls you. It begins with a practical confidence in that way of being saved which the gospel opens before you. It begins with simply trusting in that "faithful saying, and worthy of all acceptation, that Christ Jesus came into the world to save sinners,"—just such sinners as you are. It begins, therefore, with what we call coming to Christ; that is, with the act of accepting him, leaning upon him, trusting in him that he is and will be all that the gospel testifies concerning him. Christ has come to you, and is waiting before you, as a Saviour from sin by expiation and free forgiveness. You can do nothing for yourself, nor can he do anything more for you, unless you trust in him. He has come to you, and is waiting before you as a teacher and guide; and his promise is, that he will be with you always in the presence of the Holy Spirit.

Do you not see, then, what it is to begin that life to which the gospel is inviting you? Do you not see that while you wait for some preparation, which you mistakenly call conversion, or which you hope to achieve by your own endeavours, while you hesitate about committing yourself, just as you are, to the divine offer of salvation just as you find that offer in the gospel, you are really "neglecting the great salvation," and are resisting the Holy Spirit? Do you not see that there is, and can be, no other way for you to begin than by trusting God's "exceeding great and precious promises" of forgiveness, of help in the conflict with sin, and of final victory and deliverance? Such a beginning of the Christian life *is* conversion. This is what we mean when we talk of coming to Christ, and this is what Christ himself means when he bids you come to him. He who thus comes to Christ is thenceforth " in Christ," and is therefore "a new creature." The question is before you, whether you will commit yourself frankly to the grace of God in Christ, and in that confidence under- take, with . full purpose of heart, the sublime work of self-discipline for an immortal life of blessedness in the love and service of God.

You begin, when you " flee for refuge to lay hold upon the hope set before you." You begin, when your heart yields to the force of that argument : " Having therefore these promises, let us cleanse ourselves from all filthiness of the flesh and spirit, perfecting holiness in the fear of God."

Have you made that beginning ? If you have not, will you begin to-day ? Come, then, for there is no real hindrance. Come, without waiting. Now let the blessed covenant, which God in Christ offers to make with you, be established for ever. You are alone with God ; kneel before him, and say, not with your lips only, but with all your heart :—

" God be merciful to me a sinner ! O God, most holy, thou hast been merciful to me. Thou hast met me a great way off, and hast called me to return and be at peace with thee. Behold what manner of love the Father hath bestowed on me, that I should be numbered with the sons of God ! Lord, I believe ; help Thou mine unbelief ! Needy and guilty as I am, I come to thy mercy-seat, that I may take the offered mercy, and may find grace to help in time of need. I come to lay hold on the hope set before me. O God, who art in Christ, reconciling the world to thyself, I come to thee ! O Lamb of God, that takest away the sin of the world, be thou in me the hope of glory ! To whom can I go but to thee, for thou only hast the words of eternal life. Let me sit at thy feet henceforth, receiving and obeying all thy words, and trusting in thy power to save. Henceforth be my life a continued conflict with my own infirmities, with the temptations that surround me, with the evil that dwells within me. O God, that forgivest my sins, give me the victory ! Let it be my experience, as it is now my humble confidence, that I can do all things through Christ who strengtheneth me ! Thou who art not willing that any should perish, and who givest the Holy Spirit to them that ask thee, here am I in my unworthiness and helplessness ; I present myself a living sacrifice to thee. Trusting in thy offers and promises, I covenant with thee that I will be no more conformed to this world, and that I will give all diligence to be transformed by the renewing of my mind, and so to prove in my experience what is thy good and perfect and acceptable will that leads me to repentance. Work thou in me of thy good pleasure, while I work out my salvation with fear and trembling ! "

CHAPTER III.

INTEGRITY AND AMIABLENESS AS RELATED TO A RELIGIOUS LIFE.

RELIGION WITHOUT GOODNESS. A TRULY CHRISTIAN MAN IS THE BETTER FOR HIS RELIGION. MORE WORTHY OF LOVE AND CONFIDENCE IN ALL THE RELATIONS OF SOCIETY. THE CULTURE OF THE SECULAR VIRTUES IS ONE PART OF THE CHRISTIAN SELF-CULTURE. HOW THESE VIRTUES ARE TO BE CULTIVATED. DIFFERENCE IN THIS RESPECT BETWEEN THE BELIEVER IN CHRIST AND THE UNBELIEVER.

" Provide things honest in the sight of all men."—ROM. XII. 17.

" Whatsoever things are true, whatsoever things are honest, whatsoever things are just, whatsoever things are pure, whatsoever things are lovely, whatsoever things are of good report; if there be any virtue, and if there be any praise, think on these things."—PHIL. IV. 8.

Integrity and Amiableness as related to a Religious Life.

STRANGELY enough, a religious life is sometimes supposed to be quite reconcilable with a most disagreeable deficiency of those social and secular virtues which may exist without the inspiration of Christian faith. Doubtless those men who think that mere good-nature, or the graceful play and impulse of natural affections, or the merely secular morality which makes an agreeable neighbour and a wholesome member of society, is an all-sufficient substitute for religion, fall into a fatal error. But, on the other hand, those who make religion an all-sufficient substitute for the many estimable and amiable qualities of which an unregenerate man is capable, and who therefore undertake to be religious men without undertaking to be good men, are equally mistaken. There is no religious delusion more gross than that of men who expect to be saved by a religiousness which cares nothing for the things which are "honest," estimable, or becoming "in the sight of all men."

No reader of the Scriptures can fail to observe how often the apostles, in their letters to " saints and faithful brethren in Christ Jesus," urge them to cultivate those ordinary human virtues which the moral sense of all men honours, and of which there may be beautiful examples among men who know nothing of Christ, or who, having heard of Christ, do not believe in him. The thing to be observed is, not that amenity of temper and of manners, or an irreproachable morality in social and civil relations, is represented as a necessary preliminary to the reconciliation of the soul with God, but that the believer in Christ, putting on Christ's likeness and exercising himself unto godliness, cannot neglect these ordinary human virtues.   Any man, however unamiable in his natural temper, and however great his need of moral reformation in order to his being loved or respected among men, may undertake to follow Christ in the confiding hope that, by the grace of God, he shall attain a perfect salvation ; and his undertaking thus to follow Christ is just what is meant by believing in Christ.   But if he does thus undertake, he commits himself, intelligently and with all his heart, to become " a new creature ; " new in respect to whatsoever things are " beautiful in the sight of all men," new in respect to whatsoever things in human conduct are true or honest, or just, or pure, or lovely, or of good report, as well as in respect to spiritual exercises and experiences.

Assuming, then, that you to whom I am speaking from this page have undertaken, or are in the act of undertaking thus to follow Christ, I have some things to say about this particular side or aspect of the Christian life. What I say will have no other purpose than to help you in a life of faith and of devout and spiritual self-discipline.

First, then, let this be distinctly understood : The interior life of the man who follows Christ, must have for one of its manifestations that character of integrity and amiableness in social and civil relations which the common moral sense of men instinctively honours. A naturally amiable temper, a good education, and the power of merely secular motives, may indeed go far towards forming such a character ; and often a man fortunately constituted by nature, brought up under salutary restraints and influences, and accustomed to cherish every honourable and amiable impulse, may be greatly beloved and honoured without any inward experience of the gospel as a renewing power. But if religion—that is, the power of the gospel applied by the Holy Spirit to renew the heart in holiness—does not find the man already formed to such a character, it must reform him, and it will. He in whom the religion which he professes to have experienced does not thus manifest itself ; —he in whom the Spirit of grace and holiness does not actually produce these ordinary human virtues,—lacks an essential part of the character which belongs to a renewed and religious man. Whatever else he may have, this deficiency vitiates his pretensions and forbids his hopes. He in whose outward life there is not, in consequence of his religious experience, more of whatsoever things are true,—that is, who is not manifestly more to be trusted and depended on in every relation,— is a deceiver. He in whose outward life there is not, in consequence of his following Christ, more of whatsoever things are serious and dignified,—that is, who is not more sure to rise above what is trifling and low,— is a deceiver. He in whose outward life there is not, in consequence of his reconciliation to God, more of whatsoever things are just,—that is, who is not more inflexibly upright in his intercourse with men,—is a deceiver. He in whose life there is not, in consequence of his being born again, more of whatsoever things are pure,—that is, whose words and actions do not indicate a growing purity of thought and feeling,—is a deceiver. He whose life does not exhibit, in consequence of the work of the Holy Spirit upon his soul, more of whatsoever things are lovely,—that is, who is not more amiable, more gentle, more patient, more kind, or who has not more of that which wins and fixes the affectionate regard of those with whom he has to do,—is a deceiver. He in whose life there is not, in consequence of his emancipation from bondage to sin, more of whatsoever things are of good report,—that is, whose outward life does not exhibit, on the whole, more of those qualities which command the approving testimony of men's moral sense,—is a deceiver. All this is too plain to need any argument.

But we may take a higher and wider view of the

connexion between the interior life of Christian faith and the cultivation of these ordinary human virtues. The culture of the secular and social virtues, the habitual study to acquire those moral qualities which are "beautiful in the sight of all men," and to acquire them, not for the sake of the secular advantages which attend them, but for their own sake, is no unimportant part of the soul's self-discipline for immortality. A truly Christian life, a life inspired and guided by the knowledge of Christ, is the life of a redeemed soul educating and training itself for God's service here, and for that boundless existence to which it is destined hereafter. Regarding religion in this light, we may say that the conscientious cultivation of these moral qualities and habits, being a part of religion, is a part of the soul's self-discipline for immortality.

It is not to be assumed that these qualities and habits, because they are in some sense a natural outgrowth of the new life within, will therefore come spontaneously and of course. A voluntary diligence, a conscientious watchfulness of effort, is necessary to the formation of a character that shall exhibit and illustrate all that is true and dignified, and just and pure, and lovely and of good report. "If there be any virtue, and if there be any praise, *think on* these things." If virtue itself be anything more than an empty name, if the distinction between that which the moral sense approves and praises, and that which it condemns and abhors, be anything more than a dream, "think on these things." Think

on them ; that is, more accurately, hold them in estimation, reckon them at their real worth.   In other words,
seek for these traits of character ; make them your study
and pursuit ; cultivate them as of inestimable value.
If you would be fully qualified for the service of God in
this life, if you would be prepared for that higher career
of service to which he calls you in the life to come,
cultivate these virtues.

But you ask, perhaps, what connexion is there
between the culture of these secular virtues, and of these
affections that have their sphere and being only in the
present life, and the discipline of my soul for the higher
career of its immortality ?   So have I known a thoughtless boy refusing to believe that the discipline and
instruction of the school had any connexion with his
being prepared for the career which he was destined to run
in the years of his manhood.   The Author of our immortal nature has placed us here for a while, in his own
wisdom, and in the prosecution of the ends for which he
gave us being ; and here, in the brief span of life, we
must be educated for an immortal career of holiness, or
else we must go to our eternity, at the end, unfitted,
and with an account to give of life misspent, and blessed
opportunities and privileges abused.   Of the life to come
we know little beyond the fact that it is, and that its
course, whether of endless and joyful advancement in
purity, love, and blessedness, or of endless darkness and
despair, is to be determined by the results of this preparatory stage of being.   But of this present life, we

know that, in one way or another, all the elements and
conditions of it are ordered and combined by infinite
wisdom, with reference to that life to come.   We know
that, however duty here may differ in its details from
duty hereafter, these duties here, all of them—the duties
which grow out of relations soon to be dissolved, the
duties which have respect to interests transient in their
nature—are *duties* not less really than the duties which
have respect immediately and exclusively to God, and
which grow directly out of our relations to him ; and
that, if performed *as duties*, they may be the best of all
methods for disciplining the soul, and training it into
fitness for the performance of higher, yet analogous and
kindred duties, in eternity.   For example : the relation
of property or possession may not exist hereafter in any
form in which we can now conceive of it ; but how easy
is it to understand that the duties growing out of this
relation here, disciplining the soul to justice, to self-
denial, to industry, to beneficence, may be essential as
a preparatory discipline for the exercise of the same
virtues in duties and relations now unknown and uncon-
ceived.   For another example : the daily household
duties that press upon us, in the homely and humble
form of care and toil for bodily support and comfort—
the father and mother feeding the children, clothing
them, guarding them from danger, ministering to them
in sickness,—may be quite unknown hereafter.   We may
even imagine that, among the members of one family on
earth, there will be in eternity no mutual dependence,

no relation of peculiar duties and affections; but who cannot see that, even in such a case, the love, the patience, the gentleness, the confidence, and the gratitude, which are learned, or ought to be learned in the family, and in the performance of the humblest family labour, may be of incalculable importance as a part of the soul's education for the exercise of the same virtues in relations of which we have now no conception, but to which our approaching change will introduce us?

Remember, then, that the devout and habitual culture of all these secular virtues, domestic, social, and civil, is essential to the soul's self-discipline for the immortal life to come.

Here we come to a view still more practical. How is such a character to be formed and cultivated? How may I promote in myself the growth of whatever in human affection and conduct is true, and whatever is noble, and whatever is just, and whatever is pure, and whatever is amiable and attractive, and whatever is of good report? The answer to this question divides itself into two parts, neither of which is complete by itself.

First, the character in question may be cultivated by cultivating the constitutional sensibilities on which it depends. These sensibilities are natural to all men, not indeed in the same degree, but in various degrees; and in all men they may be cultivated, or they may be suppressed. There is in all men, for example, a natural sensibility to whatsoever things are true, a sensibility which is the foundation of the virtue of mutual fidelity

among men. There is a sensibility in your nature
prompting you to fulfil your engagements. Whatever
you know that your dependants, your friends, your
fellow-men in whatever relation, may reasonably expect
of you, *that* the sensibility I speak of prompts you to
do. The sensibility may be stronger in you, naturally,
than it is in some men ; it may be weaker than it is in
some other men ; but, in one degree or another, it is an
element of your constitution, and of the constitution of
every human being. This sensibility may be cultivated
and developed, till it shall move as with the precision
and force of an instinct ; and, on the other hand, it may
be resisted, kept under, and suppressed, till you shall
become almost unconscious of it. In like manner (to
take another example) you are so constituted by the
Author of your nature that you feel yourself moved—
not irresistibly impelled, but moved—to whatsoever
things are amiable, kind, and winning. All men have
naturally the same feeling, not in the same degree, but
in various degrees, according to the individual peculiarities
with which they are born. In you, in all men, this
sensibility may be cultivated and increased, or may be
stifled and suppressed.

These sensibilities are suppressed, subdued, and in a
measure extinguished, by being resisted and counteracted.
No fact in the natural history of the human mind is
more familiarly known than this. Every natural sen- '
sibility may be gradually extinguished by resistance and
by disuse. The robber, at first, struggled against his

inborn sense of justice to bring himself to the crime
which he meditated; but, by familiarity with crime,
that better sensibility, which at first revolted at the
thought of plundering his neighbour, grows faint and
ineffective.   So each of the human sensibilities related
to these secular virtues may be deadened by habitual
suppression, or by the habitual indulgence of antagonist
passions.   You may resist the impulse which moves you
to whatsoever things are true; and, by the resistance,
the spring from which that impulse comes is weakened.
You may refuse to act in accordance with the impulse
which moves you to act in accordance with whatsoever
things are honourable, and at each refusal that impulse
loses somewhat of its power.   You may hold back from
whatsoever things are demanded by an ingenuous sense
of justice, or from whatsoever things are pure, or lovely,
or of good report; and all those things will become,
gradually yet infallibly, more and more alien to your
nature.   Just so, on the other hand, these impulses, by
yielding to them and bringing to their aid the power of
habit, may be made continually more effectual.   Let
your thoughts be *accustomed* to observe, and your will
to honour with its free homage, the beauty of whatsoever
things are true, or honest, or just, or lovely, or of good
report; and the sensibilities which recognise these things
and move you to pursue them, will become more vivid,
more distinct, more prompt and powerful in their
impulse on the soul.   Think on these things.   Cultivate the sense of their worth and their beauty.   Let the

habits of your mind be formed to *obey* these sensibilities ; be careful to allow in yourself nothing that is unamiable, ungenerous, or mean, and you will find that you are training yourself to do, as if by an unconscious instinct, whatsoever things are true, or dignified, or just, or pure, or lovely, or of good report.

But I do not forget that I am dealing with you to help you in the beginning and progress of a religious life. I say then, secondly, that the secular and social virtues which I am now commending to your attention, cannot be cultivated in their due relation to the Christian life and spirit, unless the natural sensibilities which prompt them are associated with higher affections. These sensibilities are a constituent part of that curiously-wrought and complicated nature which was created in the image of God. They are a portion of that nature which was designed to attain its highest dignity and blessedness in the conscious service of God, and in a willing conformity to him. These sensibilities, therefore, can have their best culture and their fairest and thriftiest growth only when they have their life in a natural and healthy connexion with nobler principles. If you would cultivate in your own conduct, amid the temptations of this world, whatsoever things are true, you must learn to adore, to fear, to love in filial confidence, the God of truth. If you would exhibit in your own character and life whatsoever things are worthy of reverent regard, you must learn to walk with God by faith, and to live in the habit of a high and blessed intercourse with him. Would you cultivate in your soul the sense and love of justice, you must find your ideal of justice in God. Would you wear the image of whatsoever is pure or lovely, you must sit at the feet of Jesus, and be led by him to the knowledge of infinite purity and infinite love.

You see what difference there is in this respect between the man who has learned to trust in Christ, as a Saviour from sin, and the man, however amiable or generous, who is living without God in the world. The latter is just what his constitutional impulses and his early education have made him, and he has no expectation of becoming better than he is. The other confesses to himself that he is not what he ought to be ; he asks to understand his errors ; he prays to be delivered even from the faults of which he is unconscious ; he is watchful against his own infirmities ; and, depending on the offers and promises of God in the gospel, he is devoutly aspiring to become like Christ, and so to be conformed to the will and image of God. In his habitual thought, all secular and social duties—all the duties of industry and fidelity, of kindness and courtesy, of justice and of mercy—are hallowed and elevated by their relation to God, to his own emancipation from sin, and to eternity. By all the discipline of duty in this life—by all the affections and responsibilities that connect him with human society— the care of a redeeming God is training him ; and he, entering into God's plan, is training himself for an immortal life of duty and of love.

Are you thus training your soul for immortality ?

CHAPTER IV.

FAITH AND MANLINESS.

WHY THE GOSPEL IS GIVEN TO YOU. ENCOURAGEMENTS TO DILIGENCE IN SELF-DISCIPLINE. FAITH WITHOUT VIRTUE—NOT NECESSARILY LICENTIOUS — MAY BE INTELLECTUAL — MAY BE SENTIMENTAL AND ÆSTHETIC. VIRTUE ADDED TO FAITH. HOW?

" Work out your own salvation with fear and trembling : for it is God which worketh in you, both to will and to do of his good pleasure."—PHIL. II. 12, 13.

" Building up yourselves on your most holy faith."—JUDE 20.

" According as his divine power hath given unto us all things that pertain unto life and godliness, through the knowledge of him that hath called us to glory and virtue : whereby are given unto us exceeding great and precious promises ; that by these ye might be made partakers of the divine nature, having escaped the corruption that is in the world through lust. And besides this, giving all diligence, add to your faith, virtue."--2 PET. I. 3-5.

Faith and Manliness.

IF you are ready to accept that salvation which is offered to you in the name of Christ; if you are ready to ask, not merely, What shall I do to be saved from the fearful looking for of judgment and fiery indignation? but also, What shall I do to be saved from sin? it will be easy to lead you, by God's help, in the right way. Your desire is to attain a truly and thoroughly Christian character; and you have made a covenant with yourself and with God that you will use all diligence to that end. What I propose, therefore, is not to argue with you, nor to expostulate, nor to ply you with exciting appeals to sensibility, but to help you, by showing you what it is which constitutes a truly and thoroughly Christian character, and by what means and endeavours you may attain to it.

Sometimes in the Scriptures the entire Christian character is summed up in a single word or phrase; such as *faith*, or *love*, or the *knowledge* of God, or *obedience* to the truth. In that mode of speech, it seems to be assumed that any one trait of holiness must of

course involve and imply every other. In other passages, we have a catalogue of Christian graces, "fruits
of the Spirit," the elements of character, which, in their
union, are Christian holiness, and which are to be sever-
ally cultivated by him who would be saved through
Christ. These two modes of speaking are by no means
inconsistent with each other. All the Christian graces
may grow naturally from one stock, and the existence of
any one of them, in reality and simplicity, may involve
the existence, in some degree, of all the rest ; and yet
each of these graces may need, in order to its growth
and its full manifestation in the life, a diligent cultivation on the part of the renewed and struggling soul.

I have already reminded you, more than once, of the
cardinal fact, that the gospel is given to you for the
express purpose of calling you, and helping you to be
saved. That fact is the reason why your salvation, from
first to last, depends on your believing the gospel. Your
believing the gospel, in the sense of accepting it and
trusting in it, implies that you are to avail yourself of
its offers. No man can really accept the gospel and
avail himself of it as a way of salvation from sin, who
does not undertake to follow Christ in newness of life.
His believing the gospel implies, of course, that he is to
build up himself on his most holy faith ; and that he is
to add to his faith virtue, or a manly well-doing.

All that God has done to save you—first by provid-
ing and proclaiming a free forgiveness through Christ,
and then by the promise and the gift of the Holy

Spirit—encourages you, and summons you to diligence, that you may make your calling and election sure. One apostle says, "Work out your own salvation with fear and trembling, *for* it is God who worketh in you." Another expands the same thought into particulars. First, The divine power has enriched us with all things necessary to spiritual life, by giving us the knowledge of a Saviour. Secondly, Christ calls us, by bringing life and immortality to light ; by setting before us glory and virtue as one and inseparable. Thirdly, There are given to us exceeding great and precious promises, that by them we, fleeing from the corruption that is in the world, may become partakers of a divine nature. Look at these several considerations, and think how they urge you to work out your own salvation in a diligent self-discipline.

Whatever pertains to life and godliness—whatever is necessary to your beginning and pursuing such a life—*that* God has given you, by giving you a knowledge of Christ. He who knows Christ, knows that there is pardon for sinners ; that a reconciliation and perpetual friendship between his own soul and the holy God is a practicable thing ; that his guilt, and all the infirmity and perverseness of which he is conscious, need not hinder him from coming to God in a penitent submission, nor from being owned of God as a forgiven and beloved child.

Christ calls you, by the glory and virtue which he sets before you. Think who calls you. He who is himself

" the brightness of the Father's glory." He who, in your nature, compassed about with human temptations like as you are, has magnified and honoured the law of perfect holiness, and who thus shows you in his own person all true glory and virtue. He calls you, not only by his word of invitation, but by his example and by his mediation. He calls you to a glory like his own : a glory not fictitious nor dependent on circumstances ; not in any way external to yourself, but the glory or virtue of true manliness : a glory which is simply the realization of the dignity and blessedness for which your spirit, with its immortal powers of thought, affection, and activity, was created : a glory which is in truth the glory of God himself shining forth from within you. Under such a call,—when Christ the Redeemer calls you, by setting before you the hope of immortal glory and virtue,—how urgently does the deep sense of what you are, and of what you may become, move you to give yourself at once to the diligent training of yourself in holiness !

There are given to you exceeding great and precious promises. What are they ? The promise of the Holy Spirit, the inward teacher, comforter, and guide of those who trust in Christ. The promise from the ascending Saviour, " Lo, I am with you always !" The promise from the bosom of Almighty love, " My grace shall be sufficient for thee ;" " I will never leave thee, nor forsake thee." The promise, " No good thing will he withhold from them that walk uprightly." Such promises are given to you, that by them, overcoming the temptations that address themselves to so many inferior sensibilities, you may escape the corruption that is in the world through lust, and may be transformed into the likeness of God's own purity and love. Having, therefore, these promises, how cogent is the inference : " Let us cleanse ourselves from all filthiness of the flesh and spirit, perfecting holiness in the fear of God."

You believe, then, the " faithful saying and worthy of all acceptation, that Christ Jesus came into the world to save sinners." Trusting in that testimony and in the exceeding great and precious promises which it includes, you desire to build up yourself on that most holy faith. The question is, How you are to build ; what you are to do in the process of working out your salvation ? You are resolved and ready to use all diligence that you may make your calling and election sure ; and the question is, how you are to do it ? You tell me that you believe the gospel, that you are not hindered by doubts on the question whether God is in Christ reconciling the world to himself ; but you ask, " What am I to do ?" Just here I meet you, in Christ's name, with an answer which cannot be disputed :—

" ADD TO YOUR FAITH VIRTUE."

Such a precept implies that, in some sense, there may be faith without virtue ; or at least that faith may be contemplated as disjoined from virtue, even when it is in some sense Christian faith. What is that faith to which virtue is not supplied ?

It is not, necessarily, a licentious religion like that antinomianism, theoretical and practical, which sometimes appears in the garb of zeal for the gospel of salvation by grace alone. It may be something more than that gross caricature of religion which satisfies itself with its own dogmas, and despises the restraints of morality. Virtue, as the word is now currently used, is often regarded as a merely negative quality,—an exemption from certain outward vices, particularly fraud and impurity. The word, however, in its ancient and proper meaning, implies much more than this ; it means something positive ; it means strength, manliness, worth. In its primitive sense, the word virtue (and also the Greek word thus translated) includes the idea of valour, or courage and strength for war,—the quality most appreciated and honoured in that state of society in which war is the chief test of manhood. Faith, then, though it happens to co-exist with outward decency and negative morality, may yet be faith without virtue. Faith without virtue, in the true sense of the words, is faith without real manliness, — faith which imparts no positive strength or worth to the soul.

Christian faith, in its largest sense, and indeed in every sense, is the opposite of infidelity, or of the unbelief which rejects Christ and the Word of God. Faith, in whatever sense, is the belief of Christian truth. Bearing this in mind, you may see more distinctly what faith is when disjoined from its proper relation to virtue.

There may be a merely intellectual state of mind,

which, under the force of tradition or authority, or in view of historical or other arguments, recognises the gospel of Christ as from God, and recognises the Scriptures as a true record of God's revelations to men, and recognises certain propositions as revealed and recorded in the Scriptures. Undoubtedly, this is faith or belief, so far as it goes. So far, it is the same thing with the faith of the humblest, most penitent, and most devoted believer. But if it go no further, it is faith without virtue,—it is dead; it is not faith in that higher and more complex sense in which the gospel tells us, " He that believeth shall be saved ;" it is not faith in that less analytic and more Christian use of the word, in which " faith is the substance of things hoped for, and the evidence of things not seen." The faith which is only orthodox, however logical, however intelligent and exact, is faith without virtue.

But faith without virtue may be something more than this. There may be a habit of mind, not simply intellectual but sentimental, which is only another style of the faith to which virtue has not been added. In the intellectual apprehension of God, the eternal source of being, the wise and beneficent Creator, the ever-present, sustaining, and guiding energy of the universe, the ruler and judge of his responsible creatures in all the worlds of his infinite empire ; in the mere idea of God as the Bible reveals him to-our faculty of knowledge,—there is something which kindles the natural sensibilities of wonder and awe, and wakens even a sluggish soul to emotion.   In the idea of eternity, and especially in the thought of a personal immortality, there is something which dilates the mind with the sense of grandeur, and thrills it with the feeling of an infinite deed.   In the thought of responsibility and of eternal retributions, there is something which compels the soul to tremble.   So in the history and character of Jesus Christ, there is something which speaks to the tenderest and the sublimest sensibilities of every human being.   No man can intelligently trace the story of redemption,—from the manger-cradle at Bethlehem to the cross and the tomb, and thence to the ascension from the Mount of Olives, —and not feel, to some extent, the power of it on his human sensibilities.   All this awakened sensibility may be added to the intellectual recognition of Christianity as historically and doctrinally true, while yet the virtue of which we are speaking is absent.   This, so far as it goes, is faith.   So far as it goes, it is identical with the faith of the humblest and holiest mind.   But all this, if it stop here, exhausting itself in mere feeling, however intense or however refined, is not faith, in that more complex sense in which faith accompanies salvation. Even at this point, though the feeling be ever so deep and strong, and ever so delightful, the mind's reception of the truth is faith only in that analytic sense in which faith is dead.   The faith of mere sentiment and emotion, as really as the faith of mere logic and doctrine, is faith without virtue, belief without true manliness.

You are to remember, then, that faith is complete,

and is really itself, only when it stands in its proper
relation to virtue, that is, when it lives in a vital connexion with true worth, with active strength, with
manliness of soul. In other words, faith is an unfinished and fragmentary, and therefore an unnatural
thing, unless to faith be added virtue. But how is it
that, when virtue is added to faith, the faith is completed and becomes itself? How is it that faith is
developed into virtue? What is the vital relation of
the one to the other?

I answer, faith *begins* to be unfolded into virtue,
when the intellectual reception of the gospel as true,
with the naturally attendant feeling, is accompanied by
the appropriate action of the moral powers. There may
be, in some sense, just conceptions or intellectual views
of things not seen ; and there may be emotions of wonder and awe, of fear, of desire, of hope, and even of
delight, while yet there is no sovereignty of right principle and purpose within the soul, no force of restraining
and controlling conscience, no action of the moral powers
in conformity with truth and obligation. But when these
sensibilities, fed by the contemplation of the truth, serve
to quicken and invigorate the conscience, and when, instead of terminating in mere emotion, they terminate in
right action, swaying the will and all the moral and responsible nature to those inclinations and affections, and
to those aims and efforts in life, which constitute true
manhood,—when thus all that the gospel reveals of
majesty and glory, of terror and mercy, of pity and of

love, begins to be the spring of action in the soul,—
then to faith is added something of virtue, and faith
begins to show itself in its completeness—not dead but
living—a vital force. Then it is, and not till then, that
faith begins to " work by love," and to take hold upon
eternal life.

The *progress* of faith, as it is unfolded into virtue,
may be delineated by tracing the progressive subjuga-
tion of the soul in all its habits to the power of conscience and to the will of God. When the soul is not
only impelled to individual acts of manliness by over-
mastering appeals, but is formed to habits of manliness
by the steady influence of eternal things upon the
thoughts and the unexcited feelings, when, through the
long-accustomed regard of things not seen, temptation
gradually loses its power, and duty is performed ; not
reluctantly, not as the result of a struggle against old
propensities, but promptly, gladly, with undivided
energy ; then virtue is added to faith. Then it is
that faith is complete, by being the source from which
the soul is supplied, unfailingly, with manly strength
for all responsibility, and with a spontaneous earnest-
ness in duty.

We are now prepared for the more immediately practical question : How, by what diligence, is this result
to be realized ? I will suppose that this question is
your question. I will suppose that you, to whom I
am speaking from this page, are asking how you may
thus build up yourself on your most holy faith ; by

what endeavours of self-discipline your belief of the gospel may be unfolded into virtue. Assuming. that you are in earnest, I will answer your question, not by propounding particular rules of self-discipline, but rather by suggesting to you some general views, which, if you receive them and act upon them, may be better to you than much minute instruction.

1. Remember, then, that to perform all the duties of your allotted place and relations in this life is the service to which God is calling you. This is the way in which you are to serve the will of God in your generation. God has made you, not for mere contemplation, not for the acquisition and enjoyment of knowledge alone, not merely to see and to know even the highest and most glorious of all themes of thought; but for something better and nobler. God has made you, not for mere feeling, and that kind of enjoyment which consists in feeling only, but for something higher and better. God has made you for work, and he has given you work to do. The end for which all your powers are given is not thought, nor emotion, but duty, —work to be done for God, the infinite and universal worker. Remember God has placed you here not merely to know and to feel, not merely to worship in prayer and praise, not merely to be enraptured with the sublime and the beautiful in God, and in his works and ways,—but to work. And what is the work which God has given you to do ? What is the work which he puts to your hand day by day ? *That* work you are to do for

him.   That work is duty, and duty—however humble
may be the sphere in which it is to be performed—
is something higher than all the activity of mere
thought, or all the rapture of emotion.   The duties of
your allotted place and relations in this world, the
work which he gives you the opportunity of ·doing,
the honest and useful work (honest because useful)
which belongs to your position as a member of the great
human family,—the whole of it, including all that you
can do to make any human being better or happier,—
is the service to which God is now calling you.   Remember this, and you will never fail to realize that the
religion of mere knowledge and intellectual belief is
worthless, and that the religion of mere sentimentalism is
no better.   Remember this ; remember that the service to
which God calls you is not mere meditation or emotion,
but duty,—duty in every relation of man to man, or of
man to God ; and all the grandeur and impressiveness
that there is in the objects of faith becomes a living
power to waken and impel the conscience.

2. Remember, that unless religion has this efficacy
upon your conscience, and through your conscience upon
your entire character, the whole apparatus and discipline
of religion is in your case a failure.   The Bible, prayer,
the Sabbath, the house of God, the preaching of the
Word, and the formal communion of God's people with
each other and with Christ, are what I mean by the
apparatus and discipline of religion.   The end at which
all these things aim is, that the soul may be brought.

under the dominion of the high and holy will of God. Subjection to God, or, what is the same thing, subjection to duty, is the only true manliness, for it is the chief end of man. Conscience, echoing the voice of God, and swaying the soul to a willing obedience ; conscience, communing with God, and drinking in light and life from the glory of his countenance ; conscience, acting not as an accuser only, to terrify the soul with a certain fearful looking for of judgment, but as guide, to lead the soul in paths of wisdom and of peace,—is the highest nobleness of man. And all religion, or rather all religiousness, whether it be the religiousness of formalism, or the religiousness of dogmatism, or the religiousness of sentimentalism ; all religious service and ceremony, all religious knowledge, all religious feeling, which does not quicken the conscience into activity and dominion in the soul, is a failure.

3. I may answer your question, then, in this one comprehensive precept : If you would build up yourself on your most holy faith, adding to your faith virtue, *walk by faith.* You say that you believe the gospel ; then let that which you believe inspire and control your daily activity. Faith, in the most analytic sense, is the knowledge and belief of things not seen. He who walks by sight, no matter how much he knows or how much he feels of things beyond the veil, he who in the daily work of life, in the toils and struggles through which the providence of God is leading him, governs himself only by considerations from the sphere of the

things which are transient and visible, will never add to his faith virtue. But if you will, from this time forward, walk by faith ; if you will henceforth bring your employments, your plans and undertakings, your hopes and aims, your pleasures and amusements, into the light of those invisible and eternal things which your belief recognises, and will govern yourself accordingly,—your faith, instead of lying fruitless and dead in the mind, a matter of mere intelligence or mere sentiment, will henceforth be a practical thing, translating thought and emotion into manly action, and finding itself completed in virtue.

CHAPTER V.

ENLIGHTENED CONSCIENTIOUSNESS.

ADD TO VIRTUE KNOWLEDGE. RELATION OF RELIGIOUS KNOW-
LEDGE TO CHRISTIAN CHARACTER. NECESSITY OF KNOWING WHAT
IS RIGHT, IN ORDER TO DO WHAT IS RIGHT. AN ILLUSTRATION
FROM THE NEW TESTAMENT. DEFECTS OF VIRTUE WITHOUT KNOW-
LEDGE. MORBID SCRUPULOUSNESS—A SERVILE SPIRIT—BIGOTRY.
WHEN VIRTUE IS COMPLETED IN KNOWLEDGE, THE PURPOSE OF
WELL-DOING IS ENLIVENED AND INVIGORATED, AND BECOMES AN
ENLIGHTENED CONSCIENTIOUSNESS.

" As concerning, therefore, the eating of those things that are offered in sacrifice unto idols, WE KNOW that an idol is nothing in the world, and that there is none other God but one. For though there be that are called gods, whether in heaven or in earth, (as there be gods many, and lords many,) but to us there is but one God, the Father, of whom are all things, and we in him ; and one Lord Jesus Christ, by whom are all things, and we by him. How-beit there is not in every man that KNOWLEDGE : for some, with conscience of the idol unto this hour, eat it as a thing offered un-to an idol ; and their conscience, being weak, is defiled."—1 COR. VIII. 4-7.

" Brethren, be not children in understanding : howbeit in malice be ye children, but IN UNDERSTANDING BE YE MEN." — 1 COR. XIV. 20.

" Be ye not unwise, but understanding what the will of the Lord is."—EPH. V. 17.

" And this I pray, that your love may abound yet more and more in KNOWLEDGE and in all judgment."—PHIL. I. 9.

" Giving all diligence, add to your faith, virtue ; AND TO VIRTUE, KNOWLEDGE."—2 PET. I. 5.

Enlightened Conscientiousness.

SSUMING now, that you humbly trust in the grace of God, and that, depending on Christ for reconciliation to God and for strength and victory in the conflict with evil, you have heartily undertaken to follow Christ in all well-doing, I ask for your serious attention while I attempt to show you another aspect of progress in the Christian life. You have undertaken a life-long work of self-discipline. You are resolved that henceforth the great business of your life shall be to do God's will, trusting in his mercy and his promised help, and so training yourself for your immortality. Thus you hope to be progressively emancipated from the power of sin, and transformed by the renewing of your mind.

Such progress cannot be achieved by mere strength of will. The purpose to do right, always and in all things, is not all that is necessary to a perfect well-doing. In order to do right, you must know what is right. The manliest, most strenuous, and most conscientious purpose will often err, unless it be guided by intelligence. It is not enough that you add to your faith virtue, your manly purpose of well-doing must be divinely enlightened.   You must

" ADD TO VIRTUE KNOWLEDGE."

If we take the word knowledge in its widest sense, there is a beautiful fitness in the conjunction of knowledge with that manly conscientiousness which is the legitimate consequence of faith in the Word of God. The man who receives the gospel as his hope, and who, with a quickened conscience and a resolute determination, undertakes to obey and follow Christ, must be, in proportion to his faculties, his opportunities, and his means of acquiring knowledge, an intelligent man.   Especially is he bound to be intelligent in the things which immediately concern his faith and duty as a follower of Christ. From the beginning of his confidence and hope, from his first experience of the work of the Holy Spirit, onward through all his progress as a believer, he is to grow in grace and in the knowledge of his Lord and Saviour. It is true that no eminent intelligence is necessary to the beginning of discipleship in the school of Christ, nothing more than the childlike belief that Christ is able to teach and to save, and the humble purpose to learn of him and to obey him ; but from that beginning the disciple follows on to know the Lord, and to know all that God has revealed to men.   True religion distinguishes itself from superstition by its alliance with light, and by its genial influence on all the powers of thought.   It says to all who receive its lessons, " Be not

children in understanding ; in malice be ye children, but
in understanding be ye men."

At present, however, let us take this word "knowledge" in a more limited meaning. The spontaneous
utterance of faith unfolding itself into virtue is in the
question which came from the heart of Saul in the hour
of his conversion : " Lord, *what* wilt thou have me to
do ?" That question was a cry for knowledge : " How
can I rightly serve thee whom I have persecuted ?" The
converted mind, turning to follow Christ in newness of
life, longs for the knowledge of all duty. Such is the
knowledge which must be added to virtue, as virtue is
added to faith.

For the sake of giving you a more definite idea of
what the knowledge is without which conscientiousness is
incomplete and unbalanced, let me illustrate my meaning
by a historic instance from the New Testament.

One great error of Judaism, in the time of Christ and
the apostles, was that, in its attention to external and
ceremonial institutions, it had lost sight of higher principles, and had ceased to honour with due regard the
eternal distinctions between right and wrong. Those
among them who aspired to eminent sanctity were extremely scrupulous about the payment of tithes and the
practice of ceremonial washings, and extremely sensitive
to the forms of sanctity as they understood it ; but withal
they were prone to neglect the weightier matters of inward purity and faithfulness, and of spiritual religion.
On the other hand, one grand characteristic of the re-

ligion taught by Christ and his apostles was, that it insisted on the universal and eternal first principle of holiness,—love to God and love to man,—love in the heart, flowing out spontaneously into all outward duties of morality and of piety. All outward performances, not springing from the perception and recognition of the great objects of faith, were worthless in the view of Christ, and of the apostles who spoke in his name and by his Spirit. Yet those who accepted the gospel, and trusted in Christ as the one Mediator between God and men, did not all throw off at once and equally their former habits of thinking. The converted Jew was often prone to think that ceremonial observances were of much importance, and to cramp the freedom of the gospel with the fetters of Jewish scrupulousness.

Thus it came to pass, that wherever there were churches consisting partly of Jews and partly of Gentiles, the relations of Christians to the superstitions of the heathen around them were complicated and often perplexing. The abhorred idolatry of the heathen was not confined to their temples, nor to acts of public and formal worship, but was mingled with all the concerns of life. When victims were slain in sacrifice at the temples, only a part of the flesh was ordinarily consumed on the altar ; another portion was reserved by the offerer to be a feast for his family and friends, either in the temple or in his own dwelling ; and another portion became the perquisite of the priest, and was often sent to be sold in the public market. Thus, and in many other ways, the Christian, and especially the converted Gentile, was surrounded by temptations to some sort of communion with idolatry ; and what he might do, and what he might not do, without contracting the guilt of idol worship, was sometimes a perplexing question. Some, especially those of Jewish birth and education, had a strong feeling as if some moral pollution was attached to the very flesh of an idol sacrifice, and would purchase nothing in the market, would eat nothing anywhere, without being first certified that it had no taint of idolatry about it. In this way they brought themselves under a yoke of bondage. Forgetting that the earth is the Lord's and the fulness thereof,—forgetting that it is not that which entereth into a man that defileth him,—their virtue, or strength of character and strenuous purpose to do right, though prompted and sustained by faith, was misdirected. Others there were who looked on the whole matter in a different view. " The idol," they said, " is nothing, and to me, therefore, the circumstance that this food which I find in the market-place, or which is set before me at the table of a friend, has been offered to an idol, is of no consequence. I do not offer it to the idol ; and in eating it, I give God thanks and commit no idolatry." This difference of views among imperfectly instructed disciples was one of the many sources of difficulty in the church at Corinth ; and the question was referred to the apostle Paul for his advice. The apostle in his answer (1 Cor. viii.), speaks of " knowledge," and the want of " knowledge" as having caused the difference. " We

E

know," he says, " that an idol is nothing in the world, and that there is none other God but one," " of whom are all things, and we in him ;" and therefore he whose mind is completely emancipated from all reverence for idols, and who eats this food merely as food, not asking any questions as to whence it came, and giving thanks through Jesus Christ to God the author of all good, is free from the guilt of idolatry. " Howbeit," adds the apostle, " there is not in every man that *knowledge ;* for some, with conscience of the idol to this hour, eat it *as* a thing offered to an idol, and their conscience being weak is defiled ;" and from that point, he proceeds to show that a good man's conduct, in such cases, should be regulated by a benevolent regard for the welfare of others.

You see, then, what I mean when I say that, if you are to advance in the moral and spiritual self-discipline to which the gospel calls you, your believing manliness in duty must be enlightened by knowledge. Those who were most scrupulous, most superstitious, most censorious, in regard to the indiscriminate use of meats sold in the markets at Corinth, had faith ; they believed in Christ ; they trusted in him for acceptance with God ; they received with full confidence the truth that God hath appointed a day in which he will judge the world in righteousness. Nor was their belief inoperative, for to faith they added virtue. Their faith was not mere theory or imagination, nor mere feeling ; it was to them the mainspring of action. They combined with it an active conscientiousness. They intended to do right, whatever it might cost them. But their Christian manliness, not being conjoined with knowledge, was incomplete ; it was virtue without guidance ; and therefore, with all their conscientiousness, and their determination to do right at all hazards, they erred, and so erred as to be deserving of censure for the dishonour which they brought on the name of Christ.

No wonder, then, that *knowledge* is so often insisted on in the Scriptures as an element of Christian character. Knowledge, wherever it is spoken of in a catalogue of spiritual graces or of spiritual gifts, means just what it means in the instance to which I have referred you for an illustration ; it means not speculative science, natural or even theological, but *moral discrimination.* Thus, when the apostle Paul prays for the Philippians that their love " may abound yet more and more in knowledge and in all judgment," it is that they " may approve things that are excellent," that they " may be sincere" (that is, reproachless, such that the sun may shine upon without discovering any flaw or fault), " and without offence till the day of Christ."

You see then, already, that as virtue is necessary to the completeness of faith, so knowledge, in the New Testament meaning of the word, is necessary to the completeness of virtue. As faith is the first element, and practical conscientiousness the second, so this knowledge is the third element in a well-proportioned Christian character. It is distinct from faith and virtue, inasmuch

as, in the analysis of character, it may be distinctly contemplated, and a lack of it is sometimes manifest where
faith and virtue are conspicuous.   Yet, if we take another view, it is in fact inseparable from faith and virtue,
and something of it must be implied in the very existence of true virtue sustained by Christian faith.   Virtue,
in the New Testament meaning of the word, is the manliness of faith, the soul's activity under the dictates and
the impulse of those moral sensibilities which faith has
quickened.   Knowledge is that illumination and enlargement of mind, that habit and disciplined faculty of moral
discrimination, which gives force and direction to virtue.
Virtue without knowledge is fragmentary ; virtue in its
just combination with knowledge is a whole, rounded
and complete.

You understand, then, what that knowledge is without which virtue, or religious conscientiousness, however
strenuous, is imperfect.   But I would have you understand more distinctly what are the defects of that imperfect virtue.   I do not imply that such virtue is only
a formal morality, for it is a virtue in which faith is
pre-supposed.   It is a living conscientiousness, inspired
and sustained by the habitual contemplation of things
not seen.   It is an earnest purpose, inspired and sustained by the habitual contemplation of God and eternity, of the soul's infinite need and infinite ruin, and of
redemption by the power and the sacrifice of Christ.
Such virtue, however feeble and however erring, implies
something of the faculty and of the habit of moral dis-

crimination, some discerning of things that are excellent, some perception of the moral relations and tendencies of actions, and some sense of the grand principles of Christian duty. But how often do we actually find such virtue erring, and missing its mark, and starving itself, and dishonouring its own name, for the lack of knowledge? Conscientiousness without knowledge may be earnest and devout, but it betrays its weakness; it is, at the best, a lame and unfinished virtue.

1. It is often characterized by a morbid scrupulousness. "*Tenderness* of conscience," says a most acute observer, "is always to be distinguished from *scrupulousness*. The conscience cannot be kept too sensible and tender; but scrupulousness arises from bodily or mental infirmity, and discovers itself in a multitude of ridiculous, and superstitious, and painful feelings." Whenever that moral discernment, which the New Testament calls knowledge, is wanting, there virtue, however conscientious and religious, is prone to exhaust itself on little things. So much of its time and thought and zeal is occupied with tithing mint, anise, and cummin— so much of its force is directed to the circumstances of duty—that it cannot expand into the graceful and commanding proportions of the perfect man in Christ Jesus.

2. Virtue without knowledge is naturally servile in its spirit. It walks in the oldness of the letter, and not in the newness of emancipated life. It brings itself under bondage to forms, and acts more from the fear of doing wrong, than from the fearless and joyous con-

sciousness of right. It lacks the inspiring sense of freedom. Confounding duty itself with the form or circumstances of duty, it moves under constraint, and cannot mount up as with wings. As it cannot see the right and the wrong in the light of the highest and most comprehensive principles, it naturally falls back upon some narrow formula, and guides itself by specific rules blindly applied. It depends upon some authority which is not the authority of God himself speaking to the soul which he has made. It asks not, simply and directly, What is right? what is the application of the law of love? what the spontaneous impulse of a soul moving in free and blessed accordance with the mind of God?—but, what is it which the Church, as taught by the fathers or by councils, pronounces wrong? or, what is it which this or that dictator to conscience prohibits? or, what is it which has been voted into the catalogue of immoralities by this or that reforming society? or, what is it which in some particular clique or circle is considered to be inconsistent with religion? Virtue without knowledge may be earnest and true, sustained by an inspiring conviction of the reality of things not seen; it may thus have a zeal which will compass sea and land with its heroic enterprises; it may have the sturdy inflexibility that will stand up against a world of opposition, that will not be daunted by the gloom of the prison, that will raise the hymn of victory at the stake amid the crackling fagots; but after all it is prone to be servile.

3. It follows that the virtue which has this defect is often, not to say always bigoted. The man who, while to faith he adds virtue, does not add to virtue knowledge, is not only naturally scrupulous in respect to his own actions, and servile in the subjection of his conscience to his leader, or his party, or to his narrow rule, but he can hardly avoid some taint of bigotry in his judgment of those whose consciences differ in anything from his. That particular form of doing a thing, those particular circumstances, just that drapery, may be, to such a man, in all his conscientiousness, the very essence of the duty, and the test by which he judges all men. If he were to neglect that form or those circumstances, he would condemn himself severely; and when he sees such neglect in others, he judges them with the same severity. As he guides his own conduct, so he judges the conduct of others, by forms, by traditions, perhaps, which he has received from those around him, and not by principles clearly discerned and freely applied.

Understanding thus the defects of virtue without knowledge, you are prepared to understand how it is that knowledge is the complement or completeness of virtue. Think what that virtue is which is combined with the faculty and habit of moral discrimination.

(1.) It is virtue enlivened and invigorated by an enlarged acquaintance with the objects of faith. There is a difference between that simple conviction of the reality of things not seen, which lies at the foundation of all Christian character, and that clear, discriminating, ex-

panded acquaintance with things pertaining to God and
salvation, which is acquired in the progress of religious
experience.   The one is faith ; the other is knowledge.
Some knowledge, some idea or conception of eternal
things as real, is indispensable to faith ; but as the
believing soul carries out its convictions, and translates
them into action, and thus follows on to know the Lord,
as, in a devout and obedient attention to God's Word,
it walks with God, and holds communion with infinite
purity, that soul grows not only in gracious affection,
but in the knowledge of our Lord and Saviour Jesus
Christ, and of course in the knowledge of all that
concerns his dignity, his office, and the salvation he
accomplishes.   Thus as virtue springs from faith, and is
nourished by it, so faith and virtue furnish the soul with
knowledge ; and the more familiarly a truly Christian
man is acquainted with Christianity as a whole, and in
all its parts, with God in his revealed majesty and holiness, with Christ in the glory which he had with the
Father before the world was, and in the glory of his
humiliation and death as a partaker of our nature, the
more will his resolute purpose to do right be instructed
and strengthened.   The virtue which has ripened into
knowledge is an earnest conscientiousness, strengthened
and cheered by familiar acquaintance with things not
seen.

(2.) It is more than this.   It is virtue enlightened
and free.   It is the virtue or manliness of a mind accustomed to regard the principles of duty and the rela-

tions and tendencies of actions. There may be a true conscientiousness, resolute and strenuous, that moves in bondage to rules inadequately comprehended by the mind, and applied without just discrimination. But as the disciple whose faith inspires and sustains his manly purpose of well-doing, advances in Christian knowledge, he becomes familiar, not with rules alone, but with grand principles of duty. He sees everywhere, in whatever work or duty, the application of that paramount law, the law of love to God and to man, the law of doing good, always and everywhere, for time and for eternity, in communion with the God of love. The more familiar he becomes with this first principle of all duty, and with its leading applications, the more accustomed he is to see, in every particular rule of right, the sanctity, and beauty of this universal law ; the more spontaneously will his sense of right distinguish the things that are excellent ; and the more effectually will he be brought into the illuminated freedom of those whose inmost life is holiness and love.

" Giving all diligence, add to your faith virtue, and to virtue knowledge." Remember this. Knowledge, the completeness of virtue, is to be attained by diligence. Remember that the disciple must give all diligence if he would build up, on the basis of his faith, a true and manly character. Remember that, in order to the completeness of virtue and of the soul's conformity to Christ, there must be a steady, earnest, persevering self-discipline. And is not the attainment worth the effort ? Think not that the attainment is too high for you. Remember those exceeding great and precious promises whereby you may escape the corruption that is in the world, and become partaker of a divine nature. Remember that those promises avail not for the indifferent and the slothful, but for those who give all diligence that they may add to their faith virtue, and to virtue knowledge.

CHAPTER VI.

FREEDOM SELF-GOVERNED.

ONE-SIDEDNESS. TWO SORTS OF ONE-SIDED MEN AT CORINTH. KNOWLEDGE WITHOUT TEMPERANCE TENDS TO SENSUAL INDULGENCE—TO CONTEMPT OF THE WEAK—TO LAX OPINIONS TERMINATING IN APOSTASY. KNOWLEDGE DEVELOPED INTO TEMPERANCE—PUTS THE DISCIPLE ON HIS GUARD AGAINST ALL SELF-INDULGENCE—MAKES HIM HUMBLE AND GENTLE — TRAINS HIS INCLINATIONS AND EMOTIONS INTO HARMONY WITH DUTY. HOW TO ACQUIRE A CHRISTIAN SELF-CONTROL.

" But take heed, lest by any means this liberty of yours become a stumbling-block to them that are weak. For if any man see thee which hast knowledge sit at meat in the idol's temple, shall not the conscience of him which is weak be emboldened to eat those things which are offered to idols ; and through thy knowledge shall the weak brother perish, for whom Christ died ?"— 1 Cor. viii. 9-11.

" You know that in the races of the stadium, though all may run, yet but one can gain the prize ;—(so run that you may win.) And every man who strives in the matches, trains himself by all manner of self-restraint ; yet they do it to win a crown of fading leaves,—we a crown that cannot fade. I, therefore, run not like the racer who is uncertain of his goal ; I fight, not as the pugilist who strikes out into the air ; but I bring my body into bondage, crushing it with heavy blows, lest, perchance, having called others to the contest, I should myself fail shamefully of the prize."— 1 Cor. ix. 24-27. (Conybeare's version.)

" Moreover, brethren, I would not that ye should be ignorant, how that all our fathers were under the cloud, and all passed through the sea. . . . But with many of them God was not well pleased ; for they were overthrown in the wilderness. Now these things were our examples, to the intent we should not lust after evil things, as they also lusted. . . . Wherefore, let him that thinketh he standeth take heed lest he fall. . . . All things are lawful for me, but all things are not expedient : all things are lawful for me, but all things edify not."—1 Cor. x. 1, 5, 6, 12, 23.

" Giving all diligence, add . . . to knowledge, temperance."— 2 Pet. i. 5, 6.

Freedom Self-Governed.

HERE is great need of watching against one-sidedness in the formation and growth of religious character. Faith is the basis of all religion ; and faith in Christ, or a simple reliance on him as the only sacrifice for sin, and a simple confidence in his promises of free and full salvation, is what makes a Christian. It is here that you are to begin. You are to receive Christ and justification before God by faith ; you are to live by faith ; you are to walk by faith ; and your faith is to save you. But, as " James, the servant of God," assures you, " faith without works is dead." The faith which does not quicken the conscience, and strengthen the soul in all well-doing, is worthless. Faith, then, or confidence in the gospel, must be completed and balanced by what the apostle Peter calls " virtue," or the strenuous purpose to perform all duty ; for otherwise it is one-sided and monstrous,—a mere perversion of faith rather than faith itself. In like manner, that resolute conscientiousness—as I have already shown you—needs the guidance and strength, and the enlargement and freedom, which come from knowledge; or it is in danger of becoming a servile and timid scrupulousness or a narrow and contentious bigotry.

I am now to warn you against one-sidedness in another direction. Even when we add to faith virtue, and to virtue knowledge, we have not yet formed the perfect man in Jesus Christ. We have, indeed, guarded the conscientious purpose to do right against the danger of becoming bigoted and timorous. We have released it from the bondage of mere forms and mechanical rules, and have brought it forth to breathe the invigorating air, and move in the cheering light of Christian freedom. But just at this point the believer seeking to form his soul by grace into the image of Christ needs another caution. He must—

" ADD TO KNOWLEDGE TEMPERANCE."

Let your mind again revert to those circumstances in the early history of the gospel, and especially of the Corinthian church, from which we have already derived an illustration of the necessity of knowledge to guide and strengthen virtue. Those believers at Corinth whose zeal against idolatry, and whose dread of the moral pollution inseparable from it, would not let them purchase what was offered in the market, or eat what was set before them at the table of a friend, unless they could first obtain positive evidence that it had no taint of idolatry about it, had added virtue to their faith. They had conjoined with their confidence in Christ an earnest purpose to do right. The practical error into which they fell was the error of strenuous virtue not rightly directed. It was the error of that conscientiousness which lacks the guidance of knowledge. Others there were in Corinth who had the knowledge in which those over-scrupulous brethren were deficient ; but for that very reason, they, on their part, needed to be put upon their guard against an opposite danger. They saw and understood that an idol is nothing in the world. They knew that it was only by the consent and act of the mind that the guilt of idol-worship could be contracted. Thus they were free from the bondage of a morbid scrupulousness. Whatever was set before them, whatever was sold in the market, they could freely eat, asking no questions for conscience' sake, and offering thanks to God the giver. They added to their virtue knowledge. But they were not, therefore, free from danger even in that matter of things offered to idols. On the contrary, their strong sense of the freedom of the gospel—that very elevation of their minds above mere forms and outward rules—involved some special perils. Let us see what those perils were, and what they must be in all similar cases.

1. The man of knowledge, in the sense in which knowledge is now spoken of, is in danger from temptations to sensual indulgence. He knows that "it is not that which goeth into the mouth that defileth a man." He knows that in mere abstinence from this or that particular kind of food, in merely denying a natural and healthy appetite

or taste, in mere fastings and vigils, or in any other self-imposed privation or infliction, there is no righteousness nor anything that can commend the ascetic to God. He knows that " every creature of God is good, and to be received with thankfulness." He is emancipated from the narrow scruples by which some men are fettered. He has overcome the slavish spirit of subjection to dead forms. The gospel is to him a law of liberty. On this side, then ; even in the direction of that knowledge which emancipates him, and of that enlargement and elevation of mind which rises above little scruples and looks exclusively to great principles,—in just this quarter, he is exposed to danger from the temptations which address themselves to his inferior nature. He is in danger of falling into practices and habits which will be more pernicious to his soul than all the over-scrupulousness of an unenlightened conscience.

It seems to have been so with some at Corinth. The apostle Paul, in his first Epistle to that church, found it necessary to caution them in this particular. He warned them against " lusting after evil things" (x. 6), and most earnestly put them on their guard against drunkenness and other gross sensualities (vi. 9-20), in comparison with which the most timid and bigoted scrupulousness would only be a trifling error. You may pity the man who is afraid to taste even of the sacramental cup lest it should happen to contain something fermented. No doubt the addition of more knowledge to his virtue would be a great improvement in his religious character.

But, on the other hand, that man who, having added to his virtue knowledge, rises far above all scruples about self-indulgence,—that man who, having learned that " Christianity is neither ascetic nor fanatic," puts the sparkling wine freely and daily to his lips, and becomes discriminating and learned in the science of good eating and good drinking, and feels that to lose anything of the daily indulgence of his cultivated and fastidious appetite is a serious encroachment on his happiness,—that man needs something else, far more than the most timid slave of petty scruples needs knowledge. While he is rejoicing in his freedom from a scruple, he is becoming the slave of a lust,—bound and led captive by habits of sensual indulgence. There are men who abstain from the use of sugar, and wear no cotton in their clothing, lest they be compromised with the guilt of slavery. There are men to whose sensitive conscience the odour of burning tobacco is as offensive as it is to unsophisticated human nostrils. We may be sorry for the weakness of their consciences,—especially if they insist that their scruples shall be a rule by which to pronounce on other men's religious sincerity. But, after all, dare we say that those men, or any others equally scrupulous in other and similar matters, need the emancipating and liberalizing influence of knowledge more than he who is enslaved to the continual use of tobacco, and cannot be persuaded to throw off his fetters, needs something better than mere knowledge ? The slave of a scrupulous conscience, much as he needs to add to his virtue knowledge, holds a position of moral dignity when compared with one who, rejoicing in the freedom which his knowledge gives him, is enslaved by a factitious appetite.

This, then, is the first danger which besets the man of knowledge, rising above petty scruples : He is in danger on the side of self-indulgence.   At the same time—

2. He is also in danger of acquiring a contemptuous feeling toward those whose consciences are more timid and sensitive than his own.   His knowledge shows him the weakness of other men's scruples ; and he is likely to have little sympathy with them on some points, at least, on which their conscientious feelings are deep and strong.   While he seems to them to be wanting in virtue, or the will to do right, they seem to him to be deficient in common sense ; and while they, perhaps, censure him in their bigotry, he, in his pride, with knowledge that " puffeth up," despises them.

Such seem to have been the reciprocal feelings of parties in the Corinthian church.   While those who fell into the error of excessive scrupulousness, in regard to things offered to idols, could hardly avoid condemning others for what seemed to them a participation in the guilt of idolatry ; some, on the other hand, of those whose knowledge emancipated them from all superstitious regard for the idol, and who felt that they could eat of anything, anywhere, in the spirit of thankfulness to the living and true God, were proud of their knowledge, and despised the weakness of their brethren.   As to the effect of their conduct on other people, what was

that to them ? " Why," said they, " is my liberty judged
of another man's conscience ?" They felt that they could
eat, even in an idol's temple, without any inward homage
to the idol ; and as long as they kept their own conscience
pure, they esteemed it of little consequence what effect
their conduct might produce on the weak minds of others.
In reference to such results, the apostle said, " Knowledge puffeth up,"—that is, inflates the mind with pride,
—" but love edifieth. And if any man think that he
knoweth anything,"—that is, if he value himself upon
his knowledge,—" he knoweth nothing yet as he ought
to know." Knowledge that has this effect is all in vain.
Alas for that man whose supposed enlargement and elevation of views has broken the chain of sympathy between him and those whom he regards as his weaker
brethren !

3. It is also to be observed that this man of knowledge is in danger of adopting lax opinions in regard to
duty, and thus gradually blunting and benumbing his
moral sensibilities till he becomes an apostate. He
thinks much of his Christian liberty, his superiority to
merely outward rules, his illumination and guidance by
great principles living within him. To him, if the heart
be right—that is, if the disposition and ultimate aim of
the mind be right—-the particulars of outward conduct
seem to be of little consequence. His religion, he says, is
of the heart and spirit ; it does not consist in conform-
ing to the customs or the prejudices of other religion
people, in wearing a particular style of dress or a parti

cular cast of countenance, in avoiding particular sorts of company or particular amusements, in going to prayer-meetings, no, nor in any special times or rules of private prayer. Surely there is danger for him. Surely he needs something for ballast to his knowledge. The danger is that his religion will be a mere ethereal essence which evaporates and is gone. The danger is that, in his self-reliance and his freedom from prejudices, he will throw himself into one temptation and another, will be conformed to this world in one particular and another, will fall into one worldly folly and another, till his devotional habits and feelings are entirely gone; till his sympathies with Christ and with Christ's work in the world, and the communion of his heart with the people of God, are broken; till his conscience, sophisticated and blinded by false reasonings, is seared; till he becomes at last an apostate from the gospel. How many instances have there been of such backsliding and ultimate apostasy, which began in petty self-indulgences and the contempt of petty scruples!

On this part of the subject, the apostle Paul warns his Corinthian friends most distinctly and impressively. He warns those who, with an undue reliance upon their knowledge and upon the consciousness of a right intention, were not afraid to sit down at an idolatrous feast, or even in the idol's temple. He warns them by the example of those Israelites who, in the journeying under Moses through the desert, were tempted into intercourse and conformity with idolaters. "All these things," he says, " happened to them for ensamples, and they are written for our admonition, upon whom the ends of the world are come. Wherefore, let him who thinketh he standeth take heed lest he fall."

These are some of the dangers which beset the man of knowledge, as the word *knowledge* is here used ; the man whose enlarged views of moral questions have freed him from the power of superstitious or unenlightened scruples. To guard him against such dangers, he needs something else ; something without which knowledge is unbalanced ; something without which his knowledge, in its highest attainments, is incomplete. . That something else is Christian Self-control. He must add to knowledge, temperance.

What, then, do I mean by Temperance ? Of course, we need not take the word in any technical or narrow sense. Temperance, as a Christian grace, is not the mere opposite of drunkenness. It is not mere abstinence from intoxicating drinks and drugs. It is not merely a wise and health-preserving moderation in the use of food and drink. The word has a broader and higher meaning. Temperance, in the Christian sense, is the habitual and manful struggle of the soul against inferior and sensual appetites. It is the purpose and habit of striving to subdue the passions. It is the quickened spirit's watching, toil, and strife to keep the body in due subjection, and to conquer the propensities that war against the soul. This, as we see at once, is a very different thing from oriental, Jewish, or monkish asceticism, and from the scrupulousness which ascetic notions generate. It does not regard the infliction of bodily penances as meritorious or holy, or as the condition or method of acceptance with God. It only sets itself in watchfulness and conflict against those temptations which assail the soul, and seek to bring it into subjection to sin, through the appetites of the inferior nature. Christian temperance is self-control, inspired by faith, animated by manly conscientiousness, and guided by knowledge.

Let us, then, call up before our thoughts, and portray to ourselves if we can, the man who, having added virtue to faith and knowledge to virtue, adds to knowledge temperance. Look at him under the influence of this disposition or habit, and see how he is guarded against the perils which beset the man to whose knowledge temperance is not added.

1. The first element in the idea of this temperance is that it puts the man on his guard against all the forms of self-indulgence. He feels, not blindly and superstitiously, but intelligently, that the indulgence of any appetite, in such a way or to such an extent as to bring him under its power, is full of peril to his soul's prosperity. He is therefore fixed upon securing, by the help of Christ, the just dominion of his spiritual nature over all inferior desires. His body, with its organs, senses, and appetites, is to him his vehicle, his instrument, his temporary tenement, not himself; and it is a great and constant care with him not to be degraded or fettered by it. The ascetic or the mystic—for asceticism and

mysticism are ordinarily related to each other—regards the body as a clog, a burden, a prison, an enemy. His theory, with the practice founded on it, puts dishonour on his Maker, and cuts him off from the sources of spiritual strength. But the believer, adding to knowledge temperance, regards the complex constitution of his mortal existence, and all the circumstances of his probation as arranged in the wisdom and the love of God. He is in the body not for the sake of penance and suffering, but that in the body he may serve his Maker : that through these senses he may become acquainted with the outward and material creation ; that by these organs he may come into active communication with the world in which God has placed him, and in which he has a work to do for God ; and that by the discipline of temptation and of suffering, which the conditions of this life involve, he may be trained for a better life to come. Thus he puts himself intelligently on his guard, lest, by the temptations incident to his residence in the body, his soul be brought into bondage.

2. As he thus adds to knowledge temperance, he grows in humility and gentleness. Habitually watchful, he becomes habitually aware of his own weakness, his dangers, and his unworthiness. He may understand, he may pity his brother's indiscriminating and unguided scrupulousness ; but he does not therefore despise that brother, nor withhold from him a brother's sympathy. That his brother is afraid of the very food which idolatrous priests have handled,—that his brother, unable to

distinguish the circumstances of an evil thing from the thing itself, hates even " the garment spotted by the flesh," and runs into weak excesses of conscientious antipathy,—does not seem to him so unreasonable, nor is it so offensive to his feelings, as the proud and self-conceited foolhardiness that rushes into perilous temptations without fear. Thus his knowledge, completed and balanced by temperance, instead of puffing him up and separating him from a salutary sympathy with less enlightened brethren, makes him more and more helpful to them. Not having lost his sympathy with them, he does not lose their confidence, and therefore he does not lose the natural and unresisted influence over them which knowledge ought to give him. His knowledge becomes, in a sense, available for their use. His intelligent habit of moral discrimination helps to guide them.

3. In proportion to his proficiency in the habit of watchful self-restraint, his inclinations and impulses, instead of controlling his judgment of what is duty, and thus blinding his conscience, become themselves subject to the rule of truth and the sense of obligation. Such is the constitution of our nature, that when the passions are held in subjection to reason and to faith, they gradually learn to bear the yoke without resistance. At first, there may be many a conflict between the holy purpose of self-denial and the untamed passion excited by temptation and struggling for the mastery over conscience. But each victory over temptation weakens the enemy within ; each effectual curbing of wayward and grovel-

ling inclinations gives the man more power of self-control ; his nature, perverted, corrupted, and in a sense deranged and disorganized by sin, recovers more and more of the just balance of his power ; he approaches ever nearer to a full experience of that apostolic benediction : " The very God of peace sanctify you wholly : and your whole spirit, and soul, and body, be preserved blameless unto the coming of our Lord Jesus Christ."

This Christian temperance—this holy and vigilant self-restraint—is what the apostle Paul commends, most seriously, to those knowing ones at Corinth, whose knowledge had inflated them, and led them into fearful perils. " Know ye not that they which run in a race, run all, but one receiveth the prize ? So run, that ye may obtain. And every man that striveth for the mastery (in the public games) is temperate in all things. Now they do it to obtain a corruptible crown, but we an incorruptible. I therefore so run, not as uncertainly ; so fight I, not as one that beateth the air : but I keep under my body, and bring it into subjection ; lest that by any means, when I have preached to others, I myself should be a castaway." Such is Paul's commentary on adding to knowledge temperance.

Let me now give you a few brief rules that may help you in your endeavour to cultivate this self-control.

(1.) Fill your mind with just views of the dignity of your nature as created in God's image, and of the grandeur of your destiny as made for immortality. Be always conscious of what you are and what you were made for.

(2.) Be watchful against occasional temptations and against the formation of self-indulgent habits. Occasional temptations carry away the unwatchful and therefore unguarded soul ; and as they come, one after another, they bind that soul, ere it is aware, as with a chain of iron. Be watchful. Have you any self-indulgent practice or habit which it would be better for you to renounce ? Have you any circle of companions whose example and whose society tempts you to self-indulgence ? When I see a young man undertaking to be a Christian, and yet spending annually a larger amount in cigars than he can afford to give away, I am afraid for him.

(3.) Embrace such opportunities of self-denial as God gives you. Opportunities of self-denial are to be found, not made. You have no need to go out of the world into a desert or a cell, in order to deny yourself. God will take care that your moral nature suffers no harm for want of opportunities to deny itself, and to bring your impulsive and wayward passions into subjection.

(4.) Keep the end of life in view, and the end of all things. This will help you in your watchfulness. This will stimulate you to seize upon every legitimate opportunity of self-denial. This will quicken your consciousness of what you are and what you are made for. To remember that your life is only a vapour, and that the visible world itself is passing away like a shadow, will take away the glare and show of the things that deceive you,—will help you to see things as they are, and to walk as in the light of an opening eternity.

CHAPTER VII.

STEADFASTNESS.

READING THE BIBLE. UNDERSTANDEST THOU WHAT THOU READEST? THE WORD "PATIENCE" IN THE NEW TESTAMENT. STEADFASTNESS A DISTINCT ELEMENT OF CHRISTIAN CHARACTER. HOW IT MAY BE ATTAINED: I. AS THE LEGITIMATE RESULT OF FAITH, VIRTUE, KNOWLEDGE, AND SELF-CONTROL; II. BY WATCHING AGAINST TEMPTATIONS TO INSTABILITY; III. BY HABITUALLY REGARDING THE THINGS WHICH ARE NOT SEEN.

" He that endureth to the end shall be saved."—MATT. X. 22.

" In your patience possess ye your souls."—LUKE XXI. 19.

" Tribulation worketh patience ; and patience, experience."—ROM. V. 3, 4.

" Strengthened with all might, according to his glorious power, unto all patience."—COL. I. 11.

" Not slothful, but followers of them who through faith and patience inherit the promises."—HEB. VI. 12.

" Cast not away therefore your confidence, which hath great recompense of reward. For ye have need of patience, that, after ye have done the will of God, ye might receive the promise."—HEB. X. 35, 36.

" Let us run with patience the race that is set before us."—HEB. XII. 1.

" Giving all diligence . . . . add to temperance, patience."—2 PET. I. 5, 6.

Steadfastness.

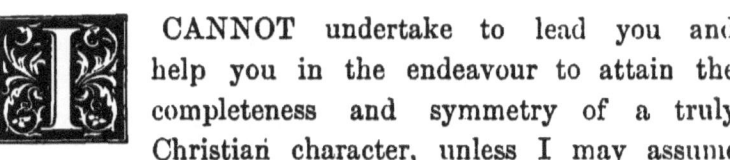

I CANNOT undertake to lead you and help you in the endeavour to attain the completeness and symmetry of a truly Christian character, unless I may assume that you are carefully and teachably reading the Bible. Such reading of the Bible, more than anything else, brings you into communication with the mind of Christ, and with the influence of the Holy Spirit. Yet, in your reading of the Bible, you may often feel the need of some friendly guidance and explanation. It will not be strange if sometimes you find yourself in sympathy with the Ethiopian courtier, who, when Philip asked him, "Understandest thou what thou readest?" replied, "How can I, except some man should guide me?"

For example, in your reading of the New Testament, you find that "patience" is frequently spoken of as something essential to the formation of a Christian character and the progress of a Christian life. What is the meaning of that word "patience," when it is thus used in the New Testament? If I can help you to a clearer understanding of that word, as it meets you so often in the reading of the Bible, perhaps I may bring your mind into a closer contact with the mind of Christ and the teaching of the Spirit.

Let me say, then, that there are two words in the New Testament which are sometimes translated *patience*. One of those two words signifies slowness to anger, indisposition to sudden resentment or complaint ; and this is very nearly what we call patience, in our ordinary use of the word. The other, which is much more frequently used in describing the Christian character and life, signifies rather what we mean by such expressions as " continuing," " holding out," " enduring," " persevering " against opposition or temptation of whatever sort. The idea of steadfastness or perseverance rarely occurs in the New Testament under any other form than this. It is the idea of enduring and holding out in the face of adverse influences. Read the words in which our Saviour explains his own parable of the sower : " They on the rock are they, which, when they hear, receive the word with joy ; and these have no root, which for a while believe, and in time of temptation fall away. And that which fell among thorns are they, which, when they have heard, go forth, and are choked with cares, and riches, and pleasures of this life, and bring no fruit to perfection. But that on the good ground are they, which, in an honest and good heart, having heard the word, keep it, and bring forth fruit with *patience*." In other words, they bring forth fruit by *persevering* in their faith, their virtue, their know-

ledge, and their earnest and watchful self-control.
Observe how the apostle Paul represents God as award-
ing eternal life to them who seek for glory and honour
and immortality " by *patient continuance* in well-doing."
That " patient continuance " is simply perseverance ;
and what the apostle says is nothing else than what
Christ himself says, using essentially the same word,
" He *that shall endure* to the end, the same shall be
saved." Just this is the " patience " which the apostle
speaks of when he says, " We glory in tribulations also,
knowing that tribulation worketh patience, and patience
experience." He and his fellow-believers, " rejoicing
in hope of the glory of God," exulted even in their
tribulations, knowing that through the grace to which
they had been introduced by faith, tribulation would be
the occasion and the means of disciplining them to
patience, or, in other words, would call them to exercise,
and thus to confirm their steadfastness in the Christian
life. They knew that from this patience or principle of
perseverance, tried and manifested by tribulation, there
would come " experience," or the experimental knowledge of the gospel, and the consequent conviction of its
truth. In the same sense of the word, it was the same
apostle's unceasing prayer for the brethren whom he
especially remembered before God, that they might be
" strengthened with all might, according to God's glorious power, to all patience and long-suffering ; " that is, to
steadfastness combined with meekness under injuries
and sorrows. So, when he gave thanks for the spiritual

prosperity and fruitfulness of those who had believed
under his ministry, he "remembered without ceasing,"
not only their "work of faith and labour of love," but
also their "patience [or steadfastness] of hope in our
Lord Jesus Christ;" for it was evidently his belief
that as works of Christian duty spring naturally from a
living faith, and as love naturally manifests itself in
labour for those beloved, so steadfastness, or an un-
wearied perseverance, is the appropriate manifestation
and result of Christian hope.   In the same sense of the
word, the believer, compassed about with the great
cloud of witnesses, is to run his appointed race "with
patience," that is, with steady perseverance, "looking to
Jesus, who, for the joy that was set before him,
endured the cross, despising the shame :"—endurance
is patience ; he was crucified without being turned from
his purpose.   Where such "patience has its perfect
work," there, in the estimation of the apostle James,
the Christian character is "perfect and entire, wanting
nothing," — as if all the graces of holiness were
formed and manifested by the discipline that tries the
believer's steadfastness.   The same writer, in another
passage, having exhorted his readers to equanimity and
cheerfulness under vexation, persecution, and the pains
of hope deferred, by reminding them of the nearness and
certainty of eternal things, proceeds to speak again of
the same "patience :" "Behold, we count them happy
who *endure*," that is, who are steadfast when tried.
"Ye have heard of the *patience* "—the steadfastness—

" of Job, and have seen "—in his case—"the end of
the Lord,"—the completion of God's plan,—" how the
Lord is very pitiful and of tender mercy." So, in the
visions of God that were granted to his servant in
Patmos, when the veil of time was torn away, and he
looked down the long reach of coming ages, he exclaimed,
once and again, as he foresaw the successive outbreaks
of the powers of darkness against the redeemed, " Here
is the *patience* and faith of the saints ! " " Here is the
patience of the saints ! Here are they that keep the
commandments of God and the faith of Jesus." That
" patience of the saints" is their constant steadfastness.

It is not strange, then, that the apostle Peter finds a
place for this " patience" in his catalogue of the qualities that make the completeness and symmetry of Christian character. Nor is it difficult to see what he means
by " patience." He means steadfastness. He means
that weight and force of purpose which holds out in the
face of all opposing influences. Having admonished his
readers not to let their faith be that maimed, dead faith
which is disjoined from the manly purpose of well-doing;
and not to let their virtue be that erring, servile, bigoted
consciousness, which is disjoined from knowledge ; and
again, not to let their knowledge be that proud, reckless,
dangerous knowledge which is disjoined from temperance,
or the purpose and habit of self-control,—he proceeds to
counsel them that to their temperance, to this combination of qualities, they add steadfastness, stability of character, the element and force of perseverance in well-doing.

G

But here, perhaps, a question arises in your mind : If
the "patience" on which the Scriptures insist so much
is nothing else than steadfastness or perseverance, how
is it that "patience" in this sense of the word is set
down distinctly as one of the elements of a Christian
character ?   How can it be made out that perseverance
is a distinct thing from faith, or virtue, or spiritual intelligence, or temperance, or godliness, or brotherly affection, or charity ?   Is it not rather something essential
to the very being of faith, of virtue, and of all the rest,
and, therefore, indistinguishable from them ? I answer :
It is true, no doubt, that the commencement of a really
Christian life does, by the grace of God, involve the certainty of its continuance to the end.   Yet this certainty
depends not on the intrinsic nature of the Christian life,
but on the gracious purpose and promise of God. There
is no contradiction and no absurdity in supposing that
there may be faith and virtue, and knowledge and temperance, and every other trait of Christian character,
and, after all, a fatal defect of perseverance.   Hence it is
that perseverance is as distinctly insisted on by the Holy
Spirit in the Scriptures, and is made as really a condition of final salvation as faith or repentance.   A man
may make ever so much proficiency for a season ; he
may advance ever so near to the goal ; but if to all this
he does not add steadfastness—if he does not continue to
the end—he falls with them who draw back to perdition.

This, however, does not complete the answer.   When
we see a man drawing back to perdition from what

seemed to be the beginning of a Christian life, we may indeed infer (and the Scriptures authorize us to infer), from the fact of his falling away, that all his religiousness was, in some respect, unsound and hollow from the beginning. In this sense, it may be admitted that a true repentance will be a persevering repentance ; a true faith will be a persevering faith ; a true discipleship will manifest itself in the end as a discipleship which endures to the end. But, at the same time, it is true that there may be faith, and with faith virtue, and with virtue knowledge, and with knowledge temperance, without all that stability which Christ and his apostles mean when they speak of " patience." There may be an instability not amounting to actual and final apostasy,—a deficiency of weight and force in the character of the man,—an unsteadiness of aim and purpose,—which weakens all the elements of Christian character. Temperance—the attempt to subdue the appetites and passions, and to bring the whole man under the control of truth—may be irregular and unsteady. Virtue—the living conscientiousness—may act now and then with power, and at other times the mind may be diverted from its purpose, and the conscience become less active and controlling. This shows us what the apostle Peter means by faith, virtue, knowledge, and temperance, without steadfastness. He means that sort of Christian character which is governed by impulses, occasions, sympathies, and excitements, rather than by the force of inflexible principles and well-formed habits. How many instances are there of that sort in every place ! How many professed disciples, who are zealous and joyful for a while in a time of general reviving, and seemingly earnest in every good word and work, but whose religious life, like the physical life of those animals which have their winter of torpor, hibernates through the interval from one revived and joyful season to another ! How many hopeful converts are there, who seem to run well for a season, but are strangely and sadly hindered ! How many who received the word with joy, and, as we thought, were adding virtue to faith, and knowledge to virtue, and temperance to knowledge, but after a while, when special excitements and sympathies had become less effective, relaxed their diligence ! How many who have no root in themselves, and so endure only for a time !

You see, then, how it is that steadfastness, or patience, is a different thing from temperance, and different from those other elements of Christian character with which it is associated. Virtue, or manly well-doing, is the legitimate attendant and the natural product or faith, and yet there may be a faith in which the element of virtue has not yet been fairly brought out. Knowledge, or the power of moral discrimination—which acts intelligently and with the sense of freedom, instead or acting in a purblind subjection to formulas—is necessary to the completeness of the virtue which springs from faith ; and virtue itself, in its own legitimate influence, leads the mind on to this sort of knowledge. Yet there may be virtue which is defective in this respect, not having been developed into knowledge; and which is, therefore, narrow, censorious, and servile. In like manner, knowledge, with all its power of discrimination, is incomplete, if it does not include a vivid sense of the duty and necessity of self-control, or if it does not actually hold in check the inferior impulses and passions; and the man who has added to virtue knowledge will naturally watch against temptations of this kind. Yet there may be knowledge to which temperance is not joined, and which is, therefore, so one-sided and unbalanced as to be dangerous, by tending to licentiousness of living. Just so temperance, or the purpose and attempt to subjugate the inferior passions, is incomplete, feeble, and fruitless, without steadfastness; and it naturally tends to complete itself by working itself out into a firm stability of soul. Yet there may be a fervent temperance, striving to discipline the desires of the flesh and of the mind, and to bring them into subjection, which, not having yet achieved its victory, is too dependent on impulses, occasions, and sympathies, and which is, therefore, fitful and unstable; a temperance to which the grace of steadfastness has not been added.

We come, then, to the more directly practical question, How shall we add to the purpose of self-control this grace of steadfastness? What method and measures can we use with ourselves to develop, in the beautiful combination of faith, virtue, knowledge, and temperance, that higher form of a symmetrical Christian character, which is seen when to all the rest is added, or rather when from all the rest there is produced, stability or perseverance, as opposed to a mere impulsiveness that moves or stops, like the wheels of the windmill that cease to revolve when the breezes are still, or that rises and falls, like the mercury in the barometer, with the variations of the atmospheric pressure. This stability is properly a distinct aim and purpose of the Christian self-discipline. This weight and firmness of character, with its steadiness of movement in the Christian life, is not to be attained without attentive effort, and may be attained by diligence in the use of the " all things necessary to life and godliness " which are given to us " through the knowledge of him that hath called us to glory and virtue."

I offer, then, these practical suggestions :—

1. Stability of Christian character is, in one sense, a natural result of faith, virtue, knowledge, and temperance, as these qualities have been heretofore illustrated. The character that is to stand immovable amid the fluctuations of external influence, like a lighthouse amid the waves, must have for its foundation a firm belief in the great disclosures which God has made concerning things eternal. On that foundation there must stand an earnest and strenuous purpose to do God's will ; a purpose that sets the whole man at work. That purpose of well-doing must enrich the mind with a practical knowledge of the great principles by which the moral sense is guided to the discernment of duty, and is emancipated from bondage to narrow, slavish, blinding for-

mulas. That knowledge, the enlightened and cultivated power of moral discernment, must put the man upon his guard against the misleading and degrading power of inferior appetites ; and, while teaching him the necessity, must train him to the habit of a free and Christian self-control. Such a character, growing up from faith into virtue, from virtue into knowledge, and from knowledge into temperance, grows naturally, though not without diligence to that end, into a steadfastness which no changes of condition, no caprices of fashion, no ebb or flow of popular opinion or popular excitement, shall be able to overcome. Remember, then, that your stability of Christian character must not be a mere appliance of external props and aids, but something intrinsic in the character itself, like the stability of an oak, that holds with a living grasp to the soil in which it grew from the acorn, and that stands the stronger for all the winds that blow upon it. Let yours be the stability of that self-balanced character which is formed by the union and cohesion of these great moral forces : faith, virtue, knowledge, temperance.

2. At the same time, it is not unimportant to say that the temptations to instability must be watchfully avoided and resisted. A little thoughtfulness will make you know what those temptations are, and how easily they beset you. Beware of them, whatever they may be in your case. Beware of a frivolous and trifling habit of mind. Many a painful instance of religious instability comes from negligence on this point. Remember

that life, in this world of probation, is a serious and
earnest affair ; and beware of those companions, those
books, those amusements, those views of life and duty,
that make you thoughtless when you ought to be in
earnest.   Know what your weaknesses are.   Know on
what side you are likely to be assailed.   Know on what
point it is that, in your mind, the principle of self-indulgence and self-pleasing is likely to prevail over the
principle of duty.   Then to that self-knowledge add a
more jealous self-watchfulness and a more resolute self-
control.   Thus temperance, in the large and Christian
sense, shall be, in the growth of your religious character,
the parent of stability and perseverance.   Self-indulgence, in one form or another—a habit of pleasing one's
self, a yielding of the mind to impulses and dispositions
that ought to be held in subjection—is the chief and
proximate cause of religious instability.   It is not by
accident, nor without a serious meaning, that the grace
of steadfastness is named by an apostle in close connexion with the grace of self-control.   Remember her
who lingered and looked back, when God's angel was
leading her to safety.   Forget the things which are behind, if you would press toward the mark for the prize.

3. Above all, let your faith, your conscientiousness,
your knowledge, your self-denial, be continually rein-
forced by the contemplation of God and of things invisible and eternal.   This habit of mind, and nothing
else when this is wanting, gives seriousness, gravity, and
immovable strength to religious purposes and affections.

CHAPTER VIII.

GODLINESS.

INTERCOURSE WITH GOD. CHRISTIANITY IS "GODLINESS." THE RE-ENTHRONEMENT OF GOD IN THE SOUL. PROGRESS FROM FAITH ONWARD. ELEMENTS OF GODLINESS: THE "FEAR OF GOD;" THE HABIT OF PRAYER; THE HABIT OF PRAISE. GODLINESS, IF GENUINE, PRESUPPOSES FAITH, VIRTUE, KNOWLEDGE, TEMPERANCE, STEADFASTNESS, AND IS THEIR VITAL POWER. HOW GODLINESS IS ADDED TO PATIENCE.

" Behold, he prayeth."—Acts ix. 11.

" Thou, when thou prayest, enter into thy closet ; and when thou hast shut thy door, pray to thy Father which is in secret ; and thy Father which seeth in secret shall reward thee openly." —Matt. vi. 6.

" Praying always with all prayer and supplication in the Spirit, and watching thereunto with all perseverance."—Eph. vi. 18.

" Continue in prayer, and watch in the same with thanksgiving."—Col. iv. 2.

" Exercise thyself unto godliness. For bodily exercise profiteth little ; but godliness is profitable unto all things, having promise of the life that now is, and of that which is to come."—1 Tim. iv. 7, 8.

" Giving all diligence, add . . . to patience, godliness."—2 Pet. i. 6.

" The doctrine which is according to godliness."—1 Tim. vi. 3.

Godliness.

THE Christian life is a life of intercourse with God. "Behold, he prayeth," as it was said of Saul when he had submitted himself to Christ, may be said of every one in whom the life of spiritual renovation and progress has begun. If you have entered on a Christian course, you have already begun to pray, believing that God is the rewarder of them who diligently seek him. You acknowledge the authority and embrace the promise of that saying, "Thou, when thou prayest, enter into thy closet ; and when thou hast shut thy door, pray to thy Father which is in secret ; and thy Father which seeth in secret shall reward thee openly." A praying man, "praying always with all prayer and supplication in the Spirit, and watching thereunto with all perseverance and supplication," is a godly man.

"In all thy ways acknowledge God." Look to him continually, cherishing the sense of your relation to him, and of his holy and loving presence ever surrounding you. Let all your undertakings be "begun, continued, and ended in him." This is godliness.

The word which in the New Testament is translated "godliness" signifies worship, or the sentiment and habit of reverence, with the added idea that is the right kind of worship. Sometimes the word is used as a name for the true religion,—the religion which acknowledges and honours the living and true God, revealed in the person of Christ his Son ; and sometimes it is used as denoting that particular trait or habit of a religious life which the word particularly describes,—the habit of recognising God, and communing with him in acts of spiritual worship.

In the former application, the word is beautifully suggestive. The religion which the gospel proclaims and establishes ; the religion to which Christ recovers men by his redeeming and renewing work ; the religion of the kingdom of God on earth ; the religion which the Church, made up of all the redeemed and holy, maintains in its faith, in its teaching and testimony, and in its practice, is godliness, the reverent knowledge and service of the living God. Coming into a world long darkened by estrangement from God and ignorance of him, it dispels that darkness by restoring the knowledge and the free and loving worship of him whose presence, seen by faith, illuminates all worlds. It re-enthrones God in human thoughts and affections. Wherever it goes, with its victories over unbelief and sin, voices as of herald angels proclaim, "Behold, the tabernacle of God is with men, and he will dwell with them, and they shall be his people, and God himself shall be with them, and be their God."

Godliness, then, in the more definite use of the word as descriptive of personal character, is nothing else than the same re-enthronement of God in an individual soul. It is that particular aspect of a Christian life which is seen in the intercourse of thought and affection between the individual soul and God. As the world lying in wickedness is a profaned and dishonoured temple which the gospel, in its progress, is to cleanse, and in which it is to re-establish God's spiritual and accepted worship, so the individual soul, in its apostate condition, is a desecrated temple ; and when the lustration of that living temple has been performed, when the fire of sacrifice has been kindled within on the re-established altar, when the thoughts and affections of that soul have become habitually fragrant to God with sweet incense of a penitent and loving worship,—that is godliness. It is the conscious intercourse of the soul with God. As distinguished from the other elements of a Christian character, it is the habit and spirit of devotion ; that state of mind in which God is consciously present, the object of trust and love, as well as of awe. It is the soul's obedience to the precept, " Pray without ceasing : in everything give thanks."

Perhaps I may show you how the habit and the living spirit of devotion are related to other elements of Christian character, by representing to you, if I can, the progress of an earnest mind, as the characteristics of the new man are successively formed in the heart and manifested in the life. The man, we will suppose, has been made to feel, with some degree of distinctness, his own estrangement from God, and his need of a Saviour who can bring him back to the fountain of light and life. To him, in that state of mind, the gospel comes. It unveils before him the character of God, the dread realities of the infinite hereafter, and the way of salvation by the reconciling blood of Christ and the renewing grace of the Holy Spirit. He receives that gospel as true ; he accepts its offers as his hope for eternity ; he yields himself to be guided by its teachings ; he becomes a believer. This is the beginning of his Christian progress. He has faith—not a merely speculative reception of the gospel, but a confidence in it—a living faith, which, from the moment of its commencement in his soul, is the commencement of a new and spiritual life. In such a faith is involved, undoubtedly, all that makes, when fully developed, a matured and completed Christian character ; just as the oak that has braved the storms of a thousand winters was once included in a tender sprout from a half-buried acorn, so tender that it might have been crushed by an infant's foot. But his faith will grow into that matured and completed Christian character, only as he gives all diligence to a course of continued and divinely guided self-discipline. To such diligence his faith is prompting him. And now as he inquires what God, what Christ would have him do, his conscience is quickened by the impulse of this new principle of faith ; his moral sense acquires new sensibility and power ; he forms not the purpose only, but

the habit also, of doing always that which he under-
stands to be the will of God ; and thus he adds to his
faith virtue.   As he pursues this course, training
himself to the habit of well-doing, his mind, already
touched and stimulated in its intellectual faculty by the
power of faith in things not seen, acquires a more
familiar acquaintance with the comprehensive principles
of duty ; and, by the practice of inquiring what is right
in order to do right, he rises above mere forms, and
narrow unintelligent rules of duty, and learns to act
under the guidance of great principles clearly discerned
and readily applied.   Thus he adds to his virtue knowledge.   Still going on toward the measure of the stature
of a perfect man in Christ, he becomes conscious that
nothing is more adverse to his progress, or tends more
to pervert his moral judgment, and to lead him through
freedom into licentiousness, than the remaining power
of those desires and impulses which reign unresisted in
the natural man.   He therefore sets himself to subdue
those desires and impulses, to get the command over
himself in all his feelings, and to bring his whole nature
into a cherished subjection to truth and God.   He adds
to his knowledge temperance.   As he becomes more
acquainted with himself and with the dangers that beset
his way, he feels more deeply that he must never parley
with temptation ; that, if he is to escape the fate of
those who draw back to perdition, he must maintain a
watchful steadfastness, and that he cannot depend on
impulses and feelings merely.   He gives all diligence to

be steadfast, unmovable, always abounding in the work of the Lord. Thus he adds to temperance patience, or holy constancy, the patience of the saints.

But this is not the complete analysis of Christian character or of Christian progress. Faith, virtue, knowledge, temperance, and constancy, must be supported and enlivened, each of them and all of them, by conscious and constant intercourse with God. To every one of them, regarded as Christian qualities, the recognition of God, as the object of the soul's confidence and homage, is essential. A holy constancy of purpose to follow Christ, and to obey his words, is impossible, without constancy of intercourse with God. He who would add to faith virtue, and to virtue knowledge, and to knowledge temperance, and to temperance steadfastness, must add to that steadfastness, and incorporate with it, the habit of reverent and affectionate communion with God, or his diligence in other respects will be to little purpose. He must

"ADD TO PATIENCE GODLINESS."

The idea of godliness as distinguished from other Christian qualities, and the relation of godliness in that sense to spiritual life and growth, may be set in a clearer light, by recollecting what particulars are included in this meaning of the word.

One part of godliness is the habitually-cherished sentiment so often spoken of in the Scriptures as "the fear of God." The godly man is one who carries in his

mind a reverent sense of what God is. He cherishes
the awing and subduing thought of his own relation to
that eternal majesty and purity. He realizes, in every
place and in every employment, the presence of that
Holiness to which all must give account. He learns to
see God in all the works of creative power and wisdom,
and to acknowledge him in all the unfolding of his
universal providence.

In a true and Christian godliness, the sentiment of
veneration toward God carries with it a sentiment of
love, or of affectionate and obedient confidence. The
"fear of God," prompted by faith, is something very
different from a slavish dread. It is a loving and
adoring awe. It has no place where there is not a confiding and cheerful complacency in God, an elevating
and inspiring fellowship with his holiness. The godly
man, he who has effectually received "the doctrine
which is according to godliness," looks up to his Father
in heaven, not in dumb terror, but with a humble trust,
a free and filial spirit, a mind rejoicing in God's power
and universal dominion ; and this is love toward God.

Prayer is a part of godliness, and is essential to it.
Mere contemplation is not godliness, nor is mere sentiment and feeling. A man may have a philosopher's
reach and depth of thought, and may meditate sublimely
on the being and the works of God, and yet not be a
godly man. He may have a poet's splendour of imagination and tenderness of sensibility ; the beauty of
God's slightest and meanest workmanship may fill his

H

eye with tears ; and yet he may come far short of
being a godly man. The devoutness of a Christian life
includes positive worship. It is not merely the flight
of lofty thought, nor the flight of raptured feeling. It
is the soul addressing itself directly and expressly to
God, in the simplicity of the belief " that God is, and
that he is the rewarder of them who diligently seek
him." The godly man regards God as his Father, to
whose kind ear he can have secret and familiar access ;
and to that Father he addresses himself in all his weakness and in all his wants.

Nor does he come to God with his petitions only ; he
has thanks, adoration, praise, to offer at the mercy-seat.
He loves to breathe out before God his reverence, his
gratitude, his confidence, and his joy, as well as his
desires and fears. The true description of this godliness
is in the Bible, full of the thoughts which godly men
have ever loved to utter in the ear of God. Surely
there is no need of my taking pains to show you, from
the examples which the Bible gives you, how large a
place there is for adoration and joyful praise in the soul's
intercourse with God.

Observe, then, how obvious is the mutual dependence
between godliness, or devoutness, and the other elements
of Christian character.

A genuine godliness is impossible, except in connexion
with the other elements of Christian life and progress,
and especially with those which have been illustrated in
the foregoing chapters. Godliness is something to be

"added" not only to faith, but to virtue, knowledge, temperance, and stability. These are, in some sort, the indispensable pre-requisites to a real and habitual communion with God. We sometimes see a man setting out to be very godly, a great example of devoutness, without conscientiousness, or moral discrimination, or self-control, or steadfastness of character. He undertakes to add to his faith godliness, omitting those graces, intermediate in the catalogue, which are the preliminary conditions of a developed and thriving godliness. He does not add to faith virtue; he has no strong and earnest conscientiousness, no fervent purpose to do always all that is right, and to avoid always all that is wrong. He does not add to virtue knowledge; he does not apply habitually in his life those great principles of evangelical obedience which make the believer free indeed. He does not add to knowledge temperance; he has never entered upon that conflict with himself by which he is to acquire the control over the passions that pervert the moral judgment, and sear the moral sensibilities of self-pleasing men. He does not add to temperance constancy; he does not combine with his attempt or profession of well-doing that steadiness of purpose, which, having once put the hand to the plough, refuses to turn back, or to look back, from the furrow; and which, instead of yielding the soul to the power of emotions changing like the wind, and of impulses fluctuating as the sea, keeps it under the direction of principle fixed as the north star. All these things he deems of little moment ; but before these, and instead of these, is to be his godliness. A devotional habit, such as it is, he holds to be the whole of Christian character. Such godliness is unreal. That man's religion is vain. He may deceive himself ; he may not be that gross, low hypocrite who knows his own hypocrisy, but, by and by, he will be found to be a pretender.

Godliness, in order to be real, must have some foundation in the character. It cannot stand by itself where other elements of Christian progress are wanting. Godliness is a renewed and holy mind manifesting itself in those affections and duties of which God is the immediate object. But will the mind exercise itself aright in those affections and duties which relate immediately to God, if virtue, knowledge, temperance, and constancy are wanting ? Godliness is the soul's communion with God. But how can a man commune with God, how can he add to his faith godliness, when his faith does not quicken his conscience to virtue, and make him alive to all his daily duties in all human relations ?— when his faith does not inform and enliven his soul with the active power of that knowledge which is the inspiration of free obedience ?—when his faith does not bring him into conflict with all the infirmities of his corrupted nature ?—when his faith imparts to his character no gravity nor constancy ? That man's devoutness, fervent as it may seem, much as he may talk of it, much as he may rejoice in it, is all pretence or all delusion.

So, on the other hand, the foregoing traits of character are of no worth, unless they lead on to godliness or are connected with it. Let there be virtue, knowledge, temperance, and constancy, all connected with faith and with each other, as they must be in a mind that is truly renewed ; and that renewed mind *will* add to them godliness, for without the habit of intercourse with God, they are all dead. In such intercourse with God, faith finds its most invigorating exercise. In such intercourse with God, conscience becomes more sensitive to evil, and more efficient in its dominion over the voluntary powers. In such intercourse with God, the soul beholding the countenance of him who is infinite purity and infinite love, is inspired with clearer perceptions of the law of love ; and enlarged with such knowledge, it learns to walk in the manly freedom of the sons of God. In such intercourse with God, the soul is strengthened for conflict with its own infirmities, and learns to strive more earnestly and more effectually for the mastery over itself. In such communion with God, the soul grows strong in the Lord and in the power of his might, and thus the believer, divinely armed and strengthened, learns to stand above dependence upon varying impulses, " steadfast, unmoveable, always abounding in the work of the Lord."

It is important, then, to a full and well-proportioned Christian growth, that while you use all diligence to make your faith complete in a manly well-doing, and your virtue in knowledge, and your knowledge in temperance, and your temperance in a Christian constancy, you use the same diligence to develop, as the completeness and

beauty of your constancy, and in vital connexion with
it, godliness, or the habit and spirit of intercourse
with God.

But here you may reasonably ask, How shall I add
to patience, godliness ?   By what care and pains may I
acquire these devotional habits of thought, of feeling,
and of action ?   How shall this element of a well-proportioned Christian character—an element so essential
to the completeness and the life of every other—be so
formed in me that it shall be self-manifested in my life ?
There is a simple way of answering such inquiries.

1. *In all thy ways acknowledge God.*   If you would
have your constancy in the Christian profession, and the
steadfastness of your well-doing, adorned and completed
in the beauty of a devotional spirit, so that your face
shall shine with an unconscious glory caught from intercourse with heaven, you must be careful to acknowledge
God in all your ways, remembering distinctly his presence
and your relations of dependence and responsibility.   Let
every duty,—not religious duties only, but duties of every
class—not great and arduous duties only, but all those
seemingly less important acts of duty which make up
so much of the labour and discipline of this life,—be performed with a distinct reference to God's will, and as
under his eye.   Let every temptation—the least as well
as the greatest—be encountered not in the unsupported
strength of a sturdy and steadfast will, not by inferior
and merely prudential considerations, but by throwing
the mind upon its consciousness of God's presence, and

its assurance of his gracious help. Thus learn by practice and experience the beauty of that rule : " Whether
therefore, ye eat or drink, or whatsoever ye do, do all to
the glory of God."

2. *Cultivate the habit of observing God in his works.*
The whole creation is full of the Creator. Eyes blinded
by unbelief can indeed explore the creation without discovering the impress of God's hand and the gleams of
his glory that linger upon everything that he has made.
But let not your eye be so heedless or so undiscerning.
Learn to see God as he reveals himself in nature. See
him in the morning and the evening ; in the beauty of
the earth, and the radiance of the sky. See him in the
swelling bud, in the opening blossom, in the fruit that
blushes as it ripens. See him in the rainbow, the shower,
the dew, the falling snow-flake. See him ; oh, where
can you not see him, if your eye be once opened to dis-
cern his glory ! Thus shall you find yourself ever more
and more encompassed with God. Nor is God to be regarded as manifested in creation only ; to the believing
mind, he is continually exhibiting himself in his works
of providence. Learn to acknowledge him as the Supreme
Disposer of events, without whom no revolution of
empire shakes and confounds the nations, and without
whom no sparrow falleth to the ground. See him in
all the changes that affect your welfare or your duties.
He gives you daily bread. He appoints your daily tasks.
He permits, for his own wise purposes connected with
your highest welfare, the temptations that make your

daily conflicts. When the floods of sorrow overwhelm you, and deep calleth to deep, it is the noise of his water-spouts that you hear, it is his waves that have gone over you. Learn to observe him, and acknowledge him in nature and in providence.

3. *Study to become more and more acquainted with God in the Bible.* See how he reveals himself there to your admiration, your confidence, your grateful affection ! See the illustrations of his goodness, his mercy, his faithfulness, his loving-kindness ! See his glory shining upon you from the face of Christ ! Trust in him. Commit yourself, in all your interests to his love and power. Fill your mind with his thoughts, as he communicates them to you in his Word. Let his affections reign in your heart. Let his in-dwelling Spirit be the life of your soul. So shall you walk with God. So shall you dwell in the secret place of the Most High, and abide under the shadow of the Almighty.

CHAPTER IX.

BROTHERLY KINDNESS.

NATURAL AFFECTIONS—THEIR PLACE IN THE FORMATION OF A
CHRISTIAN CHARACTER. BROTHERLY KINDNESS IN THE NEW TES-
TAMENT. THE CHRISTIAN SELF-DISCIPLINE ADDS TO GODLINESS
BROTHERLY KINDNESS. GODLINESS WITHOUT HUMAN SYMPATHIES
—ITS DEFECTS AND DANGERS. HEALTHFUL INFLUENCE OF HUMAN
SYMPATHIES ON THE RELIGIOUS LIFE.

" Be kindly affectioned one to another with brotherly love."—ROM. XII. 10.

" As touching brotherly love, ye need not that I write unto you ; for ye yourselves are taught of God to love one another."—1 THESS. IV. 9.

" Seeing ye have purified your souls in obeying the truth through the Spirit unto unfeigned love of the brethren, see that ye love one another with a pure heart fervently."—1 PET. I. 22.

" Put on therefore, as the elect of God, holy and beloved, bowels of mercies, kindness, humbleness of mind, meekness, long-suffering ; forbearing one another, and forgiving one another, if any man have a quarrel against any : even as Christ forgave you, so also do ye."—COL. III. 12, 13.

" Giving all diligence, add . . . to godliness, brotherly kindness."—2 PET. I. 5, 7.

Brotherly Kindness.

ITHOUT natural affection" is the lowest deep of human degradation. It is always to be assumed, in dealing even with the most hardened of outcasts from society, that however insensible he may be to moral obligation and to the fear of God, there is somewhere within him a remnant of natural affection. If it turn out otherwise, if there be no lingering memory of mother or sister, living or dead, of father or brother, of wife or child, of teacher or friend, which can be wakened into tenderness, there is no hope for him ; he is more than "twice dead ; " his moral nature is "plucked up by the roots ; " for these natural affections, the ties of sympathy and instinctive love which bind us to each other in the special relations of human society, are at once the earliest and the latest of the divinely-provided restraints on human selfishness—the earliest to be felt, the latest to lose their power.

It would be strange, then, if those natural affections had no place or part in the formation of a Christian character, and the progress of the Christian life. It would be strange if we did not find the apostles, in those Scriptures which have come down to us from them, warning us against " bitterness, and wrath, and anger, and clamour, and evil-speaking," and whatever tends to disturb the interchange of kindly feeling in the relations that constitute families, and friendships, and neighbour-hoods, and churches, and commonwealths, and exhorting us to "put on, as the elect of God, holy and beloved, deep feelings of sympathy, kindness, humbleness of mind, meekness, long-suffering, forbearing one another, and forgiving one another, if any man have a complaint against any." It would be strange if we did not find them counselling husbands and wives, parents and chil-dren, masters and servants, to an affectionate well-doing in the relations that bind them to each other. Most of all would it be strange if we did not find them, and the Master, too, insisting with special distinctness on the affection which naturally springs up between fellow-disciples, partakers in a common salvation, worshipping at the same mercy-seat, working together in the same blessed service, and recognising each other as brethren in Christ. If you would " grow in grace, and in the knowledge of our Lord and Saviour," you must take care not to be wanting in this element of the Christian character and of the Christian life.

The term " brotherly kindness," or " brotherly love," as used in the New Testament, seems to mean social affection or sympathy, as that principle of human nature is elevated and sanctified by grace in the believer, and particularly as it exists among believers in their relation to each other. I need not undertake to prove that there is such a principle in human nature as God made it ; a principle of special kindness and sympathy between those who are specially connected with each other in the bonds that constitute society; a principle by which those who are brought into such relations, whether in the family or in the neighbourhood, whether in the daily studies and sports of childhood or in the daily labours of maturer years, whether as inhabitants of the same village or as citizens in the same commonwealth,—are bound together, not merely in the sympathies of a common humanity and the vague sentiment of philanthropy, but in ties of special affection. That there is such a principle in our nature, and that God must have designed it for a good purpose, is too obvious to be disputed. Whether this principle of special attachment can be analysed into other and simpler elements, is a question of no consequence here. Let it suffice that there is such a principle, and that it belongs to our nature by the will of our Creator. This principle, elevated and sanctified by the grace of God, and especially in the form of that special affection which springs up between Christian believers in their relation to each other as members of the household of faith, is what is meant in the New Testament by "brotherly kindness," or "brotherly love."

You, then, if you would " live godly in Christ Jesus," must take care that your godliness be completed and adorned, by adding to it brotherly kindness. For the guidance of those who undertook to be Christians when Christianity was new, it was not enough to admonish them that their reception of the gospel should not be left incomplete, by being without virtue, or a resolute and conscientious purpose to do right; that their conscientiousness should not be misguided, by being without the enlightening and emancipating effect of knowledge; that their knowledge should not be permitted to make them reckless and self-indulgent, by being without temperance or manly self-control; that their temperance should not be the fluctuating conflict with inclination, which it will be if it be temperance without steadfastness; that their steadfastness should not be mere strength of will or force of habit, as it must be, unless, by being conjoined with godliness, it becomes a steadfast walking with God;—it was also needful to admonish them that their godliness or devoutness should not be without the softening influence of social affection and sympathy.

Is it then possible that godliness, or even what seems to be godliness, may be separated from brotherly kindness? Ought we not rather to presume that, inasmuch as man is made for society, and is connected with his fellow-men around him by instinctive affections, piety towards God must of course be social; and that the separation of it from social sympathies and duties cannot really be? In some sense, doubtless, it is true that worship asks for society and sympathy; yet, in another sense, the godliness or devoutness of the recluse, who

shuts himself up for the sake of being religious alone, is
not altogether unnatural. That particular trait or habit
of a religious life which we distinguish by the name of
godliness, is the intercourse of the soul with God. It is
the soul looking up to God, habitually, in veneration,
love, prayer, praise. In a word, it is worship. And
wherever worship is really offered—whether in the wilderness or in the city, whether in the closet or in the
great congregation—it is nothing else than the thoughts
and emotions of individual minds, offered, consciously
and directly, to God. All that there is in united worship to guide and quicken the mind is without effect,
unless the mind thus quickened and guided does itself,
as an individual worshipper, address to God its own
thought and emotion. All is in vain, unless the individual mind, by its own act, is brought into communication with God, not *through* the minister or the congregation, but directly. Devoutness, then, or worship, which
is what we mean by godliness as an element in a religious life, may easily tend to withdraw itself from social
affections and duties. Inasmuch as private devotion, or
the solitary communion of the soul with God, is a necessary preparation for public worship ; and, on the
other hand, a participation in public worship, if it be
true and fervent, sends the worshipper back to his retirement, there to renew and pursue his personal intercourse
with Heaven ; we need not wonder if sometimes the
devout man begins to feel as if no duty were to be
thought of in comparison with the duty of prayer and

meditation, and as if the one great business of his life were to contemplate, with adoring thoughts, the manifestations of God in revelation and in nature.   When his mind has fallen into such a habit, he will naturally begin to feel, ere long, as if his human affections and sympathies, and the relations which bind him to society, were a disadvantage to him ; as if solitude were better than society for his religious progress and enjoyment ; and as if he ought to withdraw as much as he may from human fellowship, that he may spend his life in waiting upon God.   Thus his religion, if such feelings continue to grow upon him, becomes unsocial.   He cherishes the dream of some retirement where he may be with God, and be responsible for no man's welfare but his own. The actual character of those around him who bear the Christian name is painfully incongruous with his ideal ; he sees no benefit to be derived from fellowship with them ; and he thinks that, if he could be freed from the entanglements of human sympathies and social duties, he could grow in grace.   His godliness is honest and earnest ; but it is one-sided, and therefore incomplete.

But what are the defects and dangers of such a godliness ?   This religion, in which the devotional sentiment is not properly united with human affections and sympathies,—this self-isolating godliness, that enjoys itself only in the shade, and lives only in its own musings,— what are its tendencies in respect to the completeness of Christian character ?   Can it attain to the stature of a perfect man in Christ ? You may learn something from an intelligent answer to this inquiry.

The most obvious answer is, that godliness, disjoined from brotherly kindness, tends to an inactive and indolent type of religion. It muses and thinks ; it kindles with the fervour of its own meditations ; it prays and adores, and mounts up as into heaven on the wings of contemplation ;—or, what is quite as likely, it walks sadly and tremblingly ; it weeps in secret places ; it sees not the light of God's countenance ; it moans over its own sorrows ; it is distressed both with some dim feeling of its own deficiencies, and with the sight of wickedness and sorrow ; it often repeats to itself, " Oh that I had wings like a dove ! for then would I fly away, and be at rest ;" but it forgets to ask, "Lord, what wilt thou have me to do ?" Disjoined as it is from human sympathies, failing to recognise the ties that connect each soul with kindred souls around, it does not feel the impulses which prompt our nature to activity, and to the putting forth of influence upon others ; or if it feels those impulses, it does not recognise them as proceeding from God, and essential to mental and spiritual health, but rather as something with which godliness has no alliance. A religion thus imperfect and one-sided is deficient in respect to usefulness. Because it lacks brotherly kindness, it tends to the neglect of that great precept,. " Let us do good to all men as we have opportunity, and especially to those of the household of faith." It is unconscious of having been kindled to shine as a light in the world. It is like a lamp lighted in a tomb and left to burn itself away.

You see, then, that such a godliness is not in harmony with the divine constitution of our nature. Godliness disjoined from the special sympathies and affections of human society, is not such a godliness as man was made for. Man was not made to think merely and to feel, but to work under the guidance of thought and the impulse of feeling. He was not made for solitude ; that judgment of his Creator, " It is not good for man to be alone," is written on every part of his complex nature. If we look at him in his relation to God, he was made not for worship merely but for service. The powers with which he is endowed,—the natural bonds which connect him with his fellow-men,—the affections and sympathies which make those bonds a joy, and cannot be suppressed without some violence done to nature,—all show that God has made man, and placed him in this world, not to worship only but to serve. That godliness, then, to which brotherly kindness in every brotherly relation has not been added as by a vital growth, is not in harmony with the nature of man, as made for activity or as made for society. Thus it soon parts with common sense ; for common sense is simply practical sense,—that kind of sense which takes things as they are, and deals with them as they are,—that kind of sense which God has given to man, as a social, active, working creature, to tell him what to do and how to do it. And when godliness, or the sentiment of devotion, has parted with common sense, it debilitates the soul instead of giving it strength ; it misleads the judgment ; it becomes itself a morbid thing ; it fails of honouring God.

Here let me tell you that the godliness which is separated from a healthy connexion with human sympathies and affections tends to all sorts of errors in religion. The whole history of religion is full of instruction on this point. Godliness without brotherly kindness is essentially enthusiastic. It lives in the element of feeling. It is imaginative and speculative. It has to do, not with the tangible and every-day realities of sober duty, but rather with the world in which it walks alone, musing, communing with itself, kindling itself into excitement for excitement's sake. Thus becoming itself unhealthy and erratic, it tends to all sorts of error. It is likely to misinterpret and misapply the Word of God ; for the glory of the Bible is that it is so wonderfully a book of common sense and common life. The recluse poring over it in his cell, separated from all human activities and duties, cannot understand it aright. The Bible was given for the support and guidance of man in society ; it was given that it might help us in the duties, cares, sorrows, perils, and conflicts of this actual human life ; and in the cell of a hermit, who has fled from the duties and the sympathies of manhood, it is as much out of place as a sun-dial in a dungeon. For the uses of that unpractical and self-secluding devotion, the Bible, in its common-sense interpretation, is altogether insufficient. And, therefore, that such devotion may find its aliment and stimulus, the Bible, studied under the guidance of a morbid imagination, is converted into a book of riddles and dreams. The devotion of the cell,—the devotion that flees from the homely sympathies and duties of society,—is the parent of mystical interpretation and of mystical theology. An exaggerated and unpractical sentiment of devotion sees every truth through a discolouring and distorting medium, and so builds up its own systems of faith, mystical or metaphysical, as far removed from any sound interpretation of the Scriptures as they are from the actual need of human nature in its appointed sphere of duty and of trial.

It will not be difficult for you to see what advantages the devotional spirit derives from its legitimate association with the sympathies and affections that belong to man in society. In what way is devoutness, or that part of religion which is the direct intercourse of the soul with God, benefited by being joined with brotherly kindness or the social affections ?

First, those social affections, ennobled and elevated by devotion, react to enliven, to guide, and to strengthen the sentiment or principle of devotion. Godliness, to which brotherly kindness has been added, says, " *Our* Father who art in heaven." It says, " Give *us* this day our daily bread." It prays, " Forgive *us* our debts, as *we* forgive our debtors." It cries, " Lead *us* not into temptation, but deliver *us* from evil." Godliness without brotherly kindness is godliness in the singular number only. It prays, it confesses, it adores, only by itself and for itself. Such godliness sees nothing, and knows nothing, save itself and God ; and, therefore, it knows neither itself nor God aright. But godliness, in its legitimate union with the sympathies and affections that belong to man in his relations to his fellow-men, strengthens itself by all the natural strength of those affections and sympathies. The feeble voice of lonely devotion swells to a manlier tone when loving hearts are mingled in household worship, or when many gathered households in the Sabbath congregation, friends and neighbours, compassed about with the same perils, struggling in the same conflicts and labours, and sharing the same joys and sorrows, fill the temple with their united songs and prayers.

Thus godliness, in its legitimate union with the social affections, becomes an active principle, and rises to a just ascendency over all the powers and habits of the soul. Instead of living in silent musings only, or in lonely communings with the Infinite, it comes forth into the sphere of human duties and sympathies, to sanctify all that it touches. When that natural sentiment of worship, which exercises itself in the immediate addresses of the soul to God, is not only enlightened and directed by Christian faith, but strengthened by being blended with the sentiment of brotherly kindness in the special relations of human society, it becomes an active force in all the soul's activity. The man whose godliness is of such a sort carries, not merely the form nor merely the savour of godliness, but something of its power, into all his intercourse with men. Familiar with Christ, through whom he finds access to God, he communes with Christ, and attains to more and more of his spirit and likeness, by following him in daily acts of brotherly kindness. He is the godly man in spirit and in truth, whose godliness is not a mere sentiment, uttering itself in prayer and song, or feeding itself in tranquil meditation, but a practical habit, blending its influence with all household love and duty, and making home a blessed sanctuary, the house of God, the gate of heaven. He is in truth the godly man whose godliness, instead of being isolated and unsympathizing, goes forth spontaneously to offer the right hand of brotherhood to fellow-worshippers and fellow-believers in Christ, loving to work with them, loving them because they love the Lord, and loving to comfort and to help them for Christ's sake. He is the godly man whose godliness mingles unaffectedly, yet powerfully, with all his friendships; who cannot but pray for his friends because he loves them, and cannot but love them the more because he prays for them. He is the godly man whose godliness, instead of being a sabbath-day godliness only, or limiting itself to some particular aspect of this complex human life, hallows all his patriotic sympathies, and guides him with a steady force in all the duties of citizenship and public spirit. This is true godliness, when the acknowledgment of God, the religious or devotional sentiment which Christ has awakened and enlightened, the feeling of worship—humbled and contrite, yet confiding; awed, yet full of hope and love—invests all the legitimate sympathies and duties of this life with the awfulness of their relation to eternity and to God, and lifts up this whole mortal life into the sphere of heavenly influences.

Learn, then, to correct in your own mind, if you find it there, that unworthy prejudice which represents religion as consisting exclusively in acts and exercises of devotion. That prejudice, so widely entertained, dis honours religion, dishonours the soul of man, dishonours God. Religion is not a separate and disconnected thing, arbitrarily appended, as it were, to the character of the man ; it is not some single act in which the effect of God's grace begins and is finished ; it is not merely some distinct series of devout actions, running like a golden thread through the complicated tissue of the man's various activity ; it is not the effect of God's grace upon some single sentiment or faculty of our fallen nature : it is a new life breathed into the soul by the renewing spirit ; a new creation, in which old things pass away and all things become new ; a continued and all-transforming process, in which the whole body, soul, and spirit, all faculties, all sensibilities, all affections and activities, are sanctified to the service and the praise of God.

CHAPTER X.

CHARITY.

THE GREAT COMMANDMENT. LOVE, OR HOLY BENEVOLENCE, IMPLIED IN EVERY ELEMENT OF CHRISTIAN CHARACTER. YET, IN ANOTHER VIEW, IT IS THE CONSUMMATION OF PROGRESS IN THE NEW LIFE. BROTHERLY KINDNESS, OR INSTINCTIVE SPECIAL AFFECTION IN SOCIAL RELATIONS, NEEDS TO BE ELEVATED, EXPANDED, AND COMPLETED BY THE SPIRIT OF UNIVERSAL LOVE. THE SELF-DISCIPLINE WHICH TRAINS THE SOUL TO CHARITY.

"Though I speak with the tongues of men and of angels, and have not charity, I am become as sounding brass, or a tinkling cymbal. And though I have the gift of prophecy, and understand all mysteries and all knowledge; and though I have all faith, so that I could remove mountains, and have not charity, I am nothing. And though I bestow all my goods to feed the poor, and though I give my body to be burned, and have not charity, it profiteth me nothing. . . . And now abideth faith, hope, charity, these three; but the greatest of these is charity."—1 COR. XIII. 1-3, 13.

"Beloved, let us love one another : for love is of God ; and every one that loveth is born of God, and knoweth God. . . . He that loveth not knoweth not God ; for God is love. . . . No man hath seen God at any time. If we love one another, God dwelleth in us, and his love is perfected in us. . . . If a man say, I love God, and hateth his brother, he is a liar : for he that loveth not his brother whom he hath seen, how can he love God whom he hath not seen ?"—1 JOHN IV. 7, 8, 12, 20.

"And above all these things put on charity, which is the bond of perfectness."—COL. III. 14.

"Giving all diligence, add . . . TO BROTHERLY KINDNESS, CHARITY."—2 PET. I. 5, 7.

Charity.

ROTHERLY kindness is always beautiful. It not only wins our sympathy, but commands respect and honour, especially when it is visibly associated with religious conscientiousness. Yet the precept, "Add to brotherly kindness charity," gives us to understand that in a completed Christian character there is a higher principle of benevolence. Charity, as the word is used in the New Testament, is the same thing with that love which is required by the great commandment, "Thou shalt love thy neighbour as thyself." It is love, not in the limited and inferior sense, not in the form of those special attachments which exist by the instinct of nature between human beings connected with each other by relations of special dependence and duty, but in the higher form of universal benevolence, love to all, without limitation or partiality. This universal benevolence, which is to brotherly kindness or the special affections what virtue is to faith, what knowledge is to virtue, what temperance is to knowledge, namely, its completeness and its security against being perverted and corrupted, is represented as the consummation and the crowning beauty of a truly Christian character. Thus the apostle Paul, having exhorted his friends at Colosse to all the acts and manifestations of brotherly kindness, or of that special affection which they owed to each other as members of the same Christian fellowship, proceeds to urge upon them the higher and more comprehensive duty of universal love. Having entreated them to " put on " sympathy, kindness, humility, meekness, slowness to anger, and readiness to forgive, he adds, " And above all these things "—that is, upon them, like a girdle—" put on charity, which is the bond of perfectness." It is of this love that the apostle John speaks when he says, " If we love one another," with a love like that with which God loved us, and in which he sent his Son to be the propitiation for our sins, " God dwelleth in us, and his love is perfected in us." Thus it is that, in the passage which above all others illustrates so beautifully the meaning of this word charity, the apostle, while insisting on the unspeakable superiority of personal holiness over all gifts, however wonderful, and showing how prophecies shall cease, and tongues shall fail, and knowledge shall vanish away, says, " Charity never faileth ; " and again, " Now abideth faith, hope, charity, these three ; " these are the permanent things, permanent as religion itself, permanent as the soul which they quicken and adorn, " but the greatest of these is charity."

Yet it is not to be supposed that because this love, or

charity, is the crowning grace of a completed Christian
character, therefore there are some forms and degrees of
Christian character in which this element is wholly wanting. On the contrary, there is no true Christian profession, no renovation to holiness, no effectual experience of
Christ's saving work, without love in this highest meaning of the word. Thus our Lord himself taught, on
many occasions, that there is no true obedience to God
where the heart does not obey that great command,
"Thou shalt love thy neighbour as thyself. Thus Paul
says, " He that loveth another hath fulfilled the law ;"
for every commandment in respect to your neighbour,
everything forbidden, and everything required, is briefly
comprehended in this saying, " Thou shalt love thy
neighbour as thyself. Love worketh no ill to his neighbour; therefore love is the fulfilling of the law." And
again, he says, " Though I speak with the tongues of men
and of angels, and have not charity, I am become as
sounding brass, or a tinkling cymbal. And though I have
the gift of prophecy, and understand all mysteries, and
all knowledge ; and though I have all faith so that I
could remove mountains, and have not charity, I am
nothing. And though I bestow all my goods to feed
the poor, and though I give my body to be burned, and
have not charity, it profiteth me nothing." All works
and sacrifices of zeal, even in the service of religion, are
worthless if they are not inspired by love. In another
way, but with the same purport, the apostle John says,
" Every one that loveth is born of God ; he that loveth

not knoweth not God, for God is love." "If a man say, I love God, and hateth his brother,"—not his brother Christian merely, but his brother man,—"he is a liar ; for he that loveth not his brother whom he hath seen, how can he love God whom he hath not seen ?" We may set it down, then, as a first principle, that there is no truly Christian character in which love, charity, universal benevolence, is not an element. Wherever there is faith, a true and active faith, it is faith that works by love. Wherever there is virtue springing from faith, it is conscience owning the obligation of the law of love. Wherever there is knowledge or moral discrimination, it is a mind enlightened and trained to see spontaneously what the law of love requires. Wherever there is a Christian self-control, it is a mind struggling against its own infirmities and passions, that it may be what God would have it be, and may thus fulfil his benevolent designs. Wherever there is the principle of Christian steadfastness, it is the perseverance of a mind in which selfish impulses and habits are progressively subdued by the new spirit within,—the indwelling spirit of God's love. Wherever there is a true communion with God in worship, it is a mind that beholds and adores the glory of God as the loving Creator and Ruler of the universe. And wherever there is a Christian brotherly kindness, it is that special affection toward members of the household of faith, or toward others in relations of special sympathy and duty, which is felt and cherished by a mind that pays its willing homage to the law of universal love. Without a mind obedient to the law which says, "Thou shalt love thy neighbour as thyself," there can be neither repentance toward God nor faith toward our Lord Jesus Christ. It will not be safe for you to forget that such charity is essential to the beginning of a Christian life, and equally essential to every stage of Christian progress.

Yet it is not the less to be remembered that charity, considered as the completeness of Christian character, "the bond of perfectness," must be the result of growth in grace. As related to other elements of Christian life and progress, it is the consummation of them all. In one who has just been converted from entire worldliness and unbelief, the new mind may naturally make itself known chiefly in the simplicity with which it relies on the reality of things not seen, and lays hold on the offers and hopes of the gospel. It may be exhibited in a new tenderness of conscience, and a manly purpose to do right,—adding to faith virtue. As it advances, it will naturally become more familiar with the principles of the new life, will see with a more prompt and accurate judgment what is right, and will act in the spirit of a larger freedom,—adding to virtue knowledge. Still advancing, it becomes acquainted with the need of a vigilant self-control, and manifests itself in the endeavour to subdue every wayward impulse, and to live and walk in the pure light of truth,—and so it adds to knowledge temperance. As the same new mind goes on from strength to strength, the disciple who was at first dependent upon

frames and feelings becomes steadfast, a firm and persevering Christian, strong in the stability of principle,—
having added to temperance patience. Then, you may
see him in another stage of his spiritual growth ; he
walks with God, day by day, in calm and heavenly intercourse ; he dwells as in the secret place of the Most
High,—for to patience he has added godliness. Observing still the progress of his character, you see that his
devoutness, instead of making him unsocial and austere,
quickens his natural sympathies with those around him,
and especially with his fellow-disciples, and the grace of
God within him shows itself in the sympathies and duties
which connect him with brethren and friends, with home
and country, with the church and with the civil commonwealth,—for he adds to godliness brotherly kindness.
Nor is this all. In that brotherly kindness there is
something more than the mere play of natural sympathies. Inasmuch as it is Christian, the brotherly kindness of a soul that walks with God, there is in it
continually something of the spirit of God's love ; and
thus brotherly kindness, in the various forms of special
sympathy and affection, grows into charity. The circles
of that love, obedient to the elastic force that shapes
them, spread and widen till they include the world. The
disciple whose conversion was first seen in the simple
faith with which he laid hold on God's word of grace
and hope, and in the humble, scrupulous, yet resolute
conscientiousness with which he set himself to the performance of all duty, stands up at last in the manifest

likeness of his Father in heaven, who maketh his sun to rise on the evil and on the good, and sendeth rain on the just and on the unjust.

I have represented all this as if it were a natural growth, and in one sense it is entirely natural. Yet you must not forget that there is another view. In all the progress of the new and spiritual nature there is need of diligence. This charity, which so beautifully completes and crowns the combination of Christian graces, cannot be attained without diligent self-culture. All spiritual growth is simply the progress which the soul makes when, forgetting the things which are behind, and reaching forth to those things which are before, it presses toward the mark for the prize of the high calling of God in Jesus Christ. Charity grows out of brotherly kindness only in that soul which, moved by the Holy Spirit and living in fellowship with Christ, is humbly and earnestly endeavouring to become continually more like God. In other minds, the instinctive sentiment which connects them with the family, with kindred and friends, with countrymen, and with associates in the same religious body, is often seen to be the antagonist of charity.

Think, then, what these instinctive affections are when separated from the spirit of universal love. In other words, what becomes of brotherly kindness, in whatever form, when charity is not added to it ? For example : What is patriotism without charity ? The love of one's own native land, and of one's own country-

men as distinguished from the men of other lands, is a
natural affection, and there is something generous in it,
as there is in every human sympathy.   But is it of
course, and always, a benevolent affection ?   Does it, of
course, expand into benevolence ?   On the contrary, is
there not in every land a vulgar and heathenish patriotism, essentially malignant in its tendency ?   In the
language of such patriotism, as in the language of ancient Rome, a foreigner is the same thing with an enemy ;
or, as in the language of ancient Greece, a foreigner
is the same thing with a barbarian. ' Such patriotism
breathes hatred and contempt toward all mankind.   How
plain is it that the instinctive human sentiment of affection toward one's own country and countrymen, instead
of being essentially benevolent, is often—nay, when de-
tached from Christian principle, is naturally—nothing
else than an extended and exaggerated selfishness, the
more odious for the grandeur of the scale on which it
operates.   So of a man's instinctive affection for his
family : how often do you see that affection, instead of
wakening the man to higher and better sentiments, and
making him feel (as his Creator designed it should make
him feel) his position in the universal family of God,
actually tending the other way, and making him more
and more selfish toward all to whom he is not bound by
this instinctive passion.   Just so the sentiment of special affection which naturally springs up among those
who hold the same religious doctrines, and cherish the
same traditions,—which makes them feel that they have

common interests, and which brings them together in a special communion both of worship and of enterprise and effort,—needs to be watched, lest it become uncharitable, narrow, bigoted, the antagonist more than the support of that higher sentiment which is kindred to the universal love of God and the infinite pity of Christ. The very sympathy of brother with brother in the same church, unless each, giving all diligence, adds to brotherly kindness charity, may degenerate into a sectarian narrowness of feeling. Who will tell us that it does not often so degenerate, till it becomes, in God's sight, hardly better or holier than the sympathy which connects the members of a political faction or of a masonic fraternity? Brotherly kindness, thus degenerate and corrupt by unhallowed separation from the principle of universal love, becomes a-most unchristian clannishness.

But, on the other hand, where the believer, walking humbly with God, and loving his brethren of the household of faith, gives diligence that he may add to brotherly kindness charity, there brotherly kindness, in all its sympathies and impulses, is hallowed and exalted by that higher principle of universal love to which it ministers. In the *church*, the kindly sympathy of brother with brother being thus ennobled, is a sympathy by which they incite each other to aspirations and works of Christ-like love. The affection which binds such an one to his own *family*, being sanctified by its alliance with the higher principle of universal love, is an affection which makes him more ready to feel for the welfare of

all ; as when a woman was once asked, " Is that your
son for whom you are so interested in his danger ?" and
she made answer, " No, but he is somebody's son."
Such an one's love of *country* swells by a natural expan-
sion into universal philanthropy : not that he loves his
country less, or is less ready to labour and to suffer for
its welfare ; but the circles of his benevolence still expand beyond the habitations of his kindred, beyond the
limits of his native land, beyond the mountains and the
seas, in fellowship with the all-embracing love of God.

By what kind of diligence, then, and in what methods,
may you make this grace of charity the completeness of
your Christian character ?

1. Cultivate the spirit of universal love, by a devout
and intelligent communion with God.   The Creator of
the universe, who has filled it with life and with riches,
and whose presence and character are everywhere manifested to the eye of faith, is the God of universal love.
The controlling and upholding power of the universe,
watching everywhere over the welfare of his creatures,
and overruling all events into subserviency to his designs,
is the God of universal love.   The holy Lawgiver and
Judge of the universe, who has hedged up the way of
sin with dreadful penalties, and who makes himself
known in all worlds as the protector of innocence and
goodness, and the adversary of wrong, is the God of
universal love.   The great Author of forgiveness and
salvation for sinners ; he who so loved the world that
he gave his only begotten Son, that whosoever believeth

on him may not perish, but may have everlasting life ; he who is not willing that any should perish, but that all should come to repentance,—is the God of universal love. Acquaint yourself, then, with God. Have communion with him in all those acts of homage and devotion which he has appointed as the modes of intercourse between earth and heaven. Behold him in all the relations in which he manifests himself to the adoring and obedient mind. Behold his glory as it shines in the person of the world's Redeemer, that so you may be changed into his image. Bring down upon your soul by prayer the Holy Spirit, which he gives to them that ask him, that so you may be elevated to fellowship with him in his thoughts and affections. So surely as God is love—eternal, universal, infinite love—so surely the soul that lives in a devout and loving intercourse with him will be adorned with the beauty of resemblance to him, and will become a partaker of the Divine nature ; for God is love, and he that dwelleth in God dwelleth in love.

2. But in order that you may have such intercourse with God, you must also discipline your soul to charity by diligent well-doing in a life of usefulness. Observe what is necessary to such a life.

Your employment in the world, whatever it may be, should be such as is in itself useful to mankind. No matter how humble, or how ill-rewarded in this world, is the daily labour by which you live ; if it is only useful, it may serve to discipline your soul in love. It

is not enough that your employment is a lucrative one,
and that with the gain which it brings you may hope
to accumulate the means of usefulness. You will never
grow into the likeness of God's charity in this way.
Your employment must be itself a daily contribution of
your labour to the great aggregate of human happiness.
Never permit yourself to be drawn, by any consideration,
into an employment or enterprise in which you cannot
have the consciousness that you are doing good. And
if you find that the occupation into which you have
entered unthinkingly, is of such a nature that it has no
tendency to promote the welfare of your fellow-men,
still more, if you find that the more you labour in it
the more are you doing to make men wicked and
wretched, you must abandon it and betake yourself to
some useful employment. Do you think that the man
whose daily activity in business goes to swell the dreadful aggregate of human guilt and sorrow, can be at the
same time adding to brotherly kindness charity ? No ;
if you would put on charity as the bond of perfectness,
your employment must be such that, in pursuing it day
by day, you may be conscious of doing good as the
servant of Him who is love. Pursue your business in
this spirit, and all your daily labour, like the service of
a ministering angel, is exalted into religion. Such
labour, in whatever station, though it be no higher than
the labour of a rag-picker in the streets, or of the bare-
footed child that sweeps a crossing, may become a blessed
ordinance by which the soul is disciplined to charity.

This, however, is not the only diligence which is necessary to a life of usefulness. Your daily employment, be it ever so useful in itself, is not a sufficient discipline for the training of your soul into conscious fellowship with God's love. Therefore God surrounds you with means and opportunities of special usefulness, additional to the general usefulness of your lawful industry. You have many opportunities of doing good, not only incidentally and in the general result of that employment by which you live, but directly and for the sake of the good to be done. In such opportunities only is there the consciousness of doing good by self-denial. You must use such opportunities in the spirit of self-denial, if you would discipline your soul to charity. Remember that word, "To do good, and to communicate, forget not." Do good, as you have opportunity, to all men. Do good, not to your own family and kindred only, not only to those of your own church or sect, not only to those of your own " order " or fraternity, not only to those of your opinion or party, not only to those of your own country, but to all men, everywhere, as you have opportunity. And how many opportunities have you of doing good to men of every sort, and of every land and lineage ? Seize these opportunities ; and so learn to open your heart, and to enlarge the sphere and reach of your affections. Thus learning freely, under God's kind discipline, and by communion with his Spirit, you may become a partaker of the Divine nature.

CHAPTER XI.

CHRISTIAN GROWTH.

A CAUTION. CHRISTIAN CHARACTER NOT A MECHANICAL STRUC-
TURE, BUT A LIVING GROWTH. MYSTERIOUSNESS OF LIFE. GROWTH
OF A HUMAN MIND FROM INFANCY. GROWTH IN GRACE, BEGINNING
WITH THE NEW BIRTH. DEPENDENCE OF GROWTH ON FOOD. "SIN-
CERE MILK OF THE WORD." RELATION OF CHRISTIAN GROWTH TO
CHRISTIAN SELF-DISCIPLINE. CONDITIONS WITHOUT WHICH THERE
CAN BE NO SPIRITUAL GROWTH.

"Abide in me, and I in you. As the branch cannot bear fruit of itself, except it abide in the vine; no more can ye, except ye abide in me. I am the vine, ye are the branches."—JOHN xv. 4, 5.

"Wherefore, lay aside all filthiness, and superfluity of naughtiness, and receive with meekness the ingrafted word, which is able to save your souls: but be ye doers of the word, and not hearers only, deceiving your own selves."—JAMES I. 21, 22.

"Wherefore, laying aside all malice, and all guile, and hypocrisies, and envies, and all evil-speakings, as new-born babes, desire the sincere milk of the word, that ye may grow thereby."—1 PET. II. 1, 2.

Christian Growth.

 HAVE been describing a religious life as a life of self-discipline. I have been showing you that the gospel, rousing you to a consciousness of your capabilities and of your need, calls you to make the most of yourself for time and for eternity ; and that it comes to your aid with infinite offers and promises. Viewing the Christian life in this particular aspect, I have been describing to you the separate features of a truly religious character, and have been showing you how one Christian habit or quality must be added to another. Perhaps I have not sufficiently guarded you against the impression that there is or may be some series of exercises by which any man, if he will only put himself through the course, may attain to any degree of religious proficiency, some drill like that by which the raw recruit is trained into familiarity with the details of soldiership. Perhaps I have not sufficiently warned you not to press too far the analogy between that progressive renovation of your soul, in conformity with a divine model, and the process of building a house, or constructing a machine, or of

hewing and chiselling a statue. Therefore would I now distinctly remind you that, from first to last, the formation of a truly Christian character is not so much a construction as it is a living growth. The Scriptures recognise, indeed, the analogy between the progress of religious improvement and the construction of a building ; they call on believers to build up themselves on their most holy faith, as well as to edify one another ; but, on the other hand, they also use, and with much greater force and variety of expression, the analogies which they find between the spiritual life, from its beginning onward, and the vital processes of nature. With them, the beginning of Christian character is a birth, an ingrafting, the sprouting of a seed : and its progress toward perfection is the growth, now of a plant from the germ to the blade, and the ear, and the full corn in the ear ; now of a branch drawing its sap from the stock, and bourgeoning into fruitfulness ; now of a human soul and body from infancy to maturity. Yet it should be observed that, when the Scriptures use the idea of growth to represent the progressive renovation of the Christian believer, the nature of that growth—as moral and spiritual, and not physical—as the result of thoughtful and diligent self-culture, and not of mere spontaneity—is never forgotten. " As the branch cannot bear fruit of itself," saith Christ, " except it abide in the vine : no more can ye, except ye abide in me." " Grow in grace, and in the knowledge of our Lord and Saviour Jesus Christ." " As new-born babes, desire the sincere milk of the word, that ye may grow thereby."

Christian growth, then, by the mysterious forces of the spiritual life, is what Christian self-culture aims at. If you enter upon that self-discipline to which Christ invites you, and in which you may expect that God, according to his promises, will work in you, of his good pleasure to will and to do, all your proficiency will be a growth in grace. Doubtless your own thoughtful diligence will be, from first to last, an essential condition of that proficiency ; yet, in all your proficiency, you will be conscious of dependence on higher forces than any force of your own will. You are to grow as the plant grows under the gardener's hand. He waters it, he watches it, he trains and prunes it ; but in all its growth there is a power at work which is not his, and which giveth the increase. Think, then, on the mysteriousness of a living growth ; for with all your diligence to put on Christ, and to train yourself into conformity with him, the same mystery will be inseparable from your growth in grace.

You look upon a new-born babe,—how helpless a creature is it, and how frail ! But that weak, helpless thing is born for progress. Guarded and fed by a care of which it is at first unconscious, it not only lives, but grows. The food provided for it by the all-providing hand of its Creator, and received into its healthy system, is mysteriously transmuted into the blood, the muscle, the nerves, the bones, the entire strength and beauty of the body it nourishes. Thus, in due time, the babe by slow degrees, quite imperceptible from day to day, grows to the stature and the strength of manhood.

Analogous to this is the growth of the mind. In that new-born babe, the mind with all its capacities undeveloped, and with fewer instincts in operation than belong to the chicken breaking from the shell, is nothing more than the germ or the folded bud of an intellectual being. What is there of thought, of desire, of volition, in that mind just entering upon this mortal life? How entire a blank is its consciousness! But from the moment in which the eye first opens to the light, from the moment in which the ear receives the first impulse of sound, from the moment in which the sense of touch first encounters resistance, from the moment in which the instinct of hunger or of pain first makes itself felt in that germ of human life, the mind begins to know, to think, to feel. In other words, it begins to receive into itself, and to incorporate into its own being, inadequately no doubt, and as it were in merely infinitesimal portions,—truth, the perceived reality of things. Thus the mind grows : —its various and marvellous capacities, which at first were folded up, as the leaves, the flower, and the fruit are folded up together in the bud, are expanded and brought out, as the leaves and blossom and then the fruit come forth to light and air from the opening bud. It is by such a growth that the mind advances. The intellectual being grows not, indeed, by the same process or the same means with the material organization which it inhabits, but by means and by a process suited to its nature. It grows by acquiring knowledge, by being warmed and expanded with emotion, by putting itself forth in choice and action. It grows by taking into itself and digesting, and so incorporating with its own existence, that manifested and perceived reality of things which we call truth. Truth is that after which the mind instinctively hungers, and by which it grows.

When once the mind has begun to receive truth into itself, and its powers have thus begun to be unfolded, it it is thenceforth for ever another thing from what it was before. With the first access of knowledge to its faculty of knowing,—with the first movement of its powers, spontaneously unfolding to meet and to receive the access of knowledge,—begins its experience as an intellectual being ; and that first experience is the beginning of its growth. Thenceforth that experience is never lost. Consciousness may not analyse it ; memory may not retain it ; no image of it may be reproduced ; yet it is not lost. All that mind's after-history proceeds from this point. Whatever that mind knows, feels, does, or is, for ever afterwards, is blended with this first experience. So every subsequent experience from moment to moment, from year to year,—every perception, thought, feeling, or action,—is a part of the mind's growth, whether for good or evil. It may be soon forgotten, and never recalled, but it is not lost ; as a part of the mind's experience, it is incorporated with the mind itself.

The body which we here inhabit, constructed as it is for temporary use, comes to the limit of its growth and strength, and then begins to decay. But the mind is of another nature. Created for immortality, it is created for unlimited progress. Its growth may be retarded or quickened, may be perverted or rightly directed ; yet it grows, and there is no reason why it may not, in some sense grow for ever. Its progress may be clogged by the infirmities of the body, or may be arrested and apparently suppressed by its decay ; but progress is the first law of the mind's existence. So long as the immortal spirit continues to think, to feel, to act, it continues to grow in some sort ; each act, each emotion, each thought, throughout its immortality, is, as it were, some little line or particle added to the previous amount of its existence.

The quality of the mind's growth depends on the quality of the nutriment by which it grows. Truth, simple and pure,—the reality of things, fairly and rightly apprehended,—is the soul's fit aliment ; and when the soul is thus fed, its growth is sound. But when the truth is mixed with false apprehensions of things, or when from whatever cause it is not fairly and simply received into the mind as truth, the growth becomes diseased, deformed, monstrous, or dwarfish. When the mind, instead of desiring the truth and accepting it, rejects it and yields itself to folly, its growth, instead of being a joyful progress from one degree of wisdom and manliness to another, is a growth in folly and madness. He

that "feedeth on wind, and followeth after the east wind,"
" daily increaseth lies and desolation." He that "feedeth
on ashes" is he whom "a deceived heart hath turned aside."

Such is the growth of the mind in general. I have
described it to you for the sake of illustrating that
Christian growth to which I would have you aspire.
That growth in grace and in the knowledge of our Lord
and Saviour Jesus Christ is the progress and development of spiritual life. It is the growth of the regenerate
soul in likeness to God, and in fellowship with him.
I say the regenerate soul, because progress presupposes a
beginning, growth presupposes a birth ; and because the
beginning of this spiritual life is not by mere nature,
but by grace, not by being born of the flesh, but by
being born of the Spirit. The soul, awaking from the
torpor of its native ungodliness, led to repentance, led to
Christ, trusting in him, and sitting at his feet to learn
of him, becomes a new creature ; and thus there begins
in that soul a new life, a life which has its being and its
blessedness in a willing subjection to God. In that life
the soul is conscious of its relation to God through
Christ, and conscious of living for eternity. The soul
thus born again is born to progress. That soul's continual experience, tasting that the Lord is gracious, is a
continual growth in grace ; a growth in which the nature
of the soul, as created for conscious and willing subjection to God, becomes more and more unfolded ; a growth
in which the soul is habitually approaching toward a
perfect conformity to God's moral image.

The food that nourishes the soul for spiritual growth is the Word of God, or, in the phrase of an apostle, "the sincere [or unadulterated] milk of the word." It is truth, such truth as is suited to sustain the soul in a life of fellowship with God. It is that truth which God has revealed concerning himself, all the gospel of his grace, and especially the true and faithful saying in which all is comprehended, "Christ Jesus came into the world to save sinners." It is the truth in its simplicity, "the sincere milk of the word;" the Word, not as conveyed by mouldy and corrupting traditions; not as coagulated by metaphysical discussion, and pressed into scientific propositions dry and hard; not as embittered, and perhaps made poisonous by controversial and sectarian passions; not as diluted by the tricks of fancy, and the deceitfulness of a heart unwilling to encounter and recognise the plain reality of things; but simply "the word which by the gospel is preached to you." In the gospel no truth is set forth merely as an abstract proposition, to be received into the understanding and to lie unproductive in the memory; but, on the contrary, every truth is given out as an appeal to conscience, or to some affection of the soul; every truth stands as a motive to repentance, to submission, to holy confidence in God, to adoration, to obedience, to love. Thus in the gospel every truth is vital, giving and sustaining life in the believing soul. He who has once "tasted that the Lord is gracious" must needs hunger and thirst after righteousness; nor can he find anything else than

the sincere milk of the Word to satisfy that craving.
" How sweet are thy words unto my taste ! " The
soul, feeding upon immortal truth, becoming more and
more familiar with what God has made known concerning himself and his eternal counsels of love ; drawing
nearer and nearer to the glory of God in Christ ; animated and inspired more and more with thoughts of
eternity and heaven, of the cross, the conflict and the
victory ; apprehending and taking in more completely
the exceeding great and precious promises ; becomes
more holy and heavenly, bears more of God's likeness,
partakes more gloriously of his nature, grows daily
toward the perfect stature and the Christ-like beauty of
its approaching immortality.

But what connexion is there between this spiritual
growth and that Christian self-discipline to which you
are invited ? Perhaps you are ready to ask whether a
vital growth is not necessarily spontaneous and unconscious, and whether this idea of Christian progress is
not simply irreconcilable with the idea of progress by
self-discipline. I have already touched upon this thought ;
but let us now return to it, and see how spiritual growth,
in all its spontaneousness and unconsciousness, may be
the result of conscious and resolute endeavour. The
idea of growth is not incongruous with the idea of
culture ; and self-culture is self-discipline.

What is the representation of the Scriptures concerning Christian progress, considered as a vital growth ?
They clearly teach us that certain conditions are neces-

sary to this spiritual growth, and those conditions are such as cannot take place unconsciously or involuntarily. "Wherefore, laying aside all malice [or wickedness], and all guile, and hypocrisies, and envies, and all evil-speakings, as new-born babes [that is, with all simplicity], desire the sincere milk of the word, that ye may grow thereby." That the Word may have its effect, the mind must be in a state to receive it and relish it, and thus to be nourished by it.

Another apostle uses another comparison to illustrate the same idea. "Wherefore lay apart all filthiness, and superfluity of naughtiness, and receive with meekness the ingrafted word, which is able to save your souls." When the vine-dresser would insert into a worthless stock a graft of fruitful and generous nature, he begins by pruning off the superfluous growth of the old stock ; he removes those worthless shoots and branches, that the graft, drawing to itself the sap and life of the stock, may have the opportunity to bring forth fruit, according to its nature, from the root which yielded no good fruit before. So if the Word of God is to be grafted effectually into your soul, and if the ingrafted Word is to live within you and bear fruit according to its nature, the process must begin with the pruning-off of the superfluous wild growth. In other language, dropping the figure, you must renounce and resist the wayward affections that reign within you by nature ; you must deny yourself ; you must overcome those habits of affection, of action, and of thought, which are contrary to truth and holiness ; and thus you must receive the Word "with meekness," that is, with a mind so simple, so calm, so humble, that wayward passions and wild affections shall not choke the Word, and cause it to become unfruitful.

Returning now to the figure which the apostle Peter uses, we find it setting forth the same idea of the conditions without which there is no spiritual growth. If you would relish the pure milk of the Word, and grow thereby, as the new-born babe lives and grows by its appropriate food, you must become like that new-born babe ; you must "lay aside all malice, and all guile, and hypocrisies, and envies, and all evil-speakings ;" you must suppress all selfish habits and impulses, all deceit and affectation, all that disposition which hungers and thirsts after the seeming and advantages of righteousness rather than after righteousness itself,—all that spirit of self-exaltation which moves you to envy, and makes another's welfare or progress less desirable to you than your own, and especially all those evil and unloving words in which the spirit of selfishness seeks to express itself. The necessary condition of the soul's growth in holiness —the condition without which the Word of God cannot be effectual to spiritual growth—is, that the soul shall diligently resist all those propensities which are contrary to the Word, and to that life which the Word nourishes. The order of nature and of grace is—the order of all experience is—" Cease to do evil ; learn to do well." You cannot learn to do well, unless you begin by ceasing to do evil.

You see, then, how it is that men may hear the Word of God and read it, may find their thoughts and feelings deeply interested in it, may even make it the subject-matter of their studies and of the profoundest speculative inquiry, and may yet remain without God in the world. It is not that there is no efficacy in the Word. It is not that the Word is not suited to their nature and capacities. It is that they will not truly and frankly cease to do evil, in order that they may learn to do well. It is that they will not repent, in order to obey. It is that they will not prune off the irregular, worthless, thorny growth of selfishness and ungodliness, in order to receive with meekness the ingrafted Word. It is that they will not lay aside all malice, and all guile, and hypocrisies, and envies, ard all evil-speakings, in order to receive the Word, and to be nourished by it into holiness. They will not receive the kingdom of God as a little child may receive it. They will not turn and become as little children. A little child in its simplicity may receive the kingdom of God. The renewing efficacy of the gospel may enter into the mind with the earliest rudiments of intellectual and moral instruction. In that little child, bending at its mother's knee to pray, and hearing from its mother's lips " that sweet story of old," how Jesus took little children into his arms and blessed them, a new and spiritual life may begin ; an infant life at first, but growing with the child's growth, and strengthening with its strength. The mind, the heart, the entire soul of that child may be moulded in all the process of growth, from infancy onward, by the power of truth quickening the sense of duty and the consciousness of relations to eternity, and by the power of God's love made manifest in Christ ; while the man of high and various intelligence, speculating profoundly and inquiring accurately, reads and hears the Word of life, and even studies it attentively, without once tasting that the Lord is gracious. The spiritual life begins even in a little child that is simply and humbly obedient to the truth ; but it can have no beginning in the maturest and most enlightened mind that will not resolutely deny ungodliness, turning with earnest purpose to obey and follow Christ.

In the same way you see how it is that in many regenerate souls (as in a charitable judgment we may presume them to be) there is so little evidence of spiritual growth. It is not because the Word cannot nourish them. It is not because the promises of God are of no validity. It is because they are not diligent to overcome and suppress that which remains within them of ungodly habits and affections. They have no adequate sense or resolution of what is necessary on their part in order that the Word with which they are fed may have its effect in causing them to grow into more of the likeness of God, and more of the beauty and strength of spiritual life. In other words, they disregard the great principle which underlies those warnings : " Quench not the Spirit ;" " Grieve not the Spirit ;" " that Holy Spirit of promise." Growth in grace, while it is in one sense spontaneous, and even unconscious, is in another sense the effect of self-culture and self-discipline.   While it is in one aspect the work of the informing Word and quickening Spirit of God, it is also, in another aspect, the achievement of the soul itself struggling in God's strength, and under his guidance, against its own corruptions.

Thus have I shown you what is necessary on your part to your spiritual growth.   You must be willing to know and to condemn your own deficiencies.   You must diligently endeavour to understand your errors, and to escape from them.   As under the eye of God, and with prayer for his illumination, you must search out your secret faults, confessing them to him, and forsaking them.   You must " purify your soul in obeying the truth through the Spirit."   So shall you " grow in grace, and in the knowledge of our Lord and Saviour Jesus Christ." Your soul shall be nourished with angels' food, the Word of God, and shall grow toward " the measure of the stature of the fulness of Christ."

CHAPTER XII.

FRUITFULNESS.

SELF-CULTURE RESULTING IN FRUITFULNESS. YOU MUST NOT CONFOUND FRUITFULNESS WITH USEFULNESS, NOR WITH ZEAL FOR DOING GOOD. SCRIPTURAL IDEA OF CHRISTIAN FRUITFULNESS ILLUSTRATED IN CHRIST'S PARABLE OF THE SOWER, IN HIS ALLEGORY OF THE VINE, IN THE APOSTLE PETER'S SYNTHESIS OF CHRISTIAN CHARACTER. PRACTICAL ERRORS IN CHRISTIAN SELF-CULTURE ARISING FROM A MISTAKEN CONCEPTION OF FRUITFULNESS.

" I am the vine, ye are the branches : he that abideth in me, and I in him, the same bringeth forth much fruit ; for without me ye can do nothing."— JOHN XV. 5.

" Herein is my Father glorified, that ye bear much fruit ; so shall ye be my disciples."— JOHN XV. 8.

" Giving all diligence, add to your faith, virtue ; and to virtue, knowledge ; and to knowledge, temperance ; and to temperance, patience ; and to patience, godliness ; and to godliness, brotherly kindness ; and to brotherly kindness, charity.   For if these things be in you, and abound, they make you that ye shall neither be barren nor unfruitful in the knowledge of our Lord Jesus Christ." 2 PET. I. 5–8.

Fruitfulness.

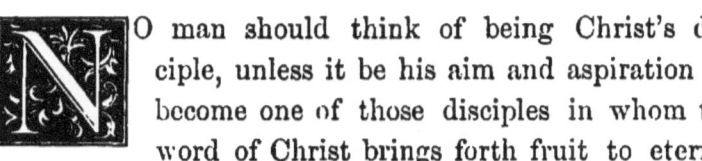O man should think of being Christ's disciple, unless it be his aim and aspiration to become one of those disciples in whom the word of Christ brings forth fruit to eternal life. Christian fruitfulness is the end for which all the means of grace are appointed, and for which grace itself is given. It is the end, therefore, of all Christian self-discipline.

What is the true idea of Christian fruitfulness? A mistaken conception of it cannot but mislead your endeavours and your aspirations. For example, if you assume that fruitfulness in the knowledge of our Lord Jesus Christ is identical with visible or traceable usefulness in the Church, you will be likely to err, not only in your judgment of yourself and of others, but also in your thoughts and hopes of Christian progress. Special usefulness is in a great measure dependent on special gifts and special opportunities. Nay, as the apostle Paul suggests, a man may be greatly useful, though in his own soul the gospel brings forth no fruit to perfection; he may preach to others with as wide a success as that which attended the Apostle of the Gentiles, and yet be himself a castaway. In like manner, if you identify the idea of fruitfulness with the one idea of *zeal* in some particular department of religious or philanthropic activity, or even with the one idea of zeal for doing good in general, as if that were the sum-total of the Christian life, your judgment of yourself and of others will be narrow and often erroneous, and your aspirations after higher attainments in personal holiness will be often misdirected.

Observe, then, carefully, what idea of Christian fruitfulness is given in the Scriptures. Begin with the parable of the sower, in which the great Teacher seems to have used this figure for the first time. His instances and illustrations of unfruitfulness are significant. First, "When any one heareth the word of the kingdom, and understandeth it not,"—that is, does not receive it into his mind,—" then cometh the wicked one, and catcheth away that which was sown in his heart. This is he which received seed by the wayside." The word of the kingdom has no effect upon him. Next, " He that received the seed into stony places, the same is he that heareth the word, and anon with joy receiveth it ; yet hath he not root in himself, but dureth for a while." The word in his case is what the seed was that fell upon stony places, springing up suddenly, but withering in the first heat, and so producing nothing. Another instance of unfruitfulness is, " he that heareth the word, and the cares of this world, and the deceitfulness of riches, choke the word, and he becometh unfruitful." The opposite of all this is fruitfulness,—the fruitfulness of him who " heareth the word and understandeth it," or takes it into his mind and digests it into thought and life,—the fruitfulness of them who " in an honest and good heart, having heard the word, keep it, and bring forth fruit with patience." Fruitfulness, according to the illustrations given in the parable of the sower, is nothing less than the entire effect of the gospel on the believing and obedient soul.

On another occasion, Christ employed a different analogy to set forth the idea of fruitfulness in his disciples. It was when he spoke of himself as the true vine, of which his Father is the husbandman, and in which his disciples are the branches. " As the branch," said he, " cannot bear fruit of itself, except it abide in the vine : no more can ye, except ye abide in me. I am the vine, ye are the branches : he that abideth in me, and I in him, the same bringeth forth much fruit : for without me ye can do nothing." " Herein is my Father glorified, that ye bear much fruit : so shall ye be my disciples,"—that is, the fact that you are indeed my disciples shall be evidenced by your fruitfulness. In this illustration, fruitfulness is nothing less than the entire effect wrought in the soul and life of the believer by that vital relation to Christ which is represented in the words, " Abide in me, and I in you."

Christian fruitfulness is mentioned in yet another connexion. Turn once more to that remarkable passage

which I have already so often commended to your attention, and in which the exceeding great and precious
promises are referred to as an encouragement to diligence
in a spiritual self-discipline. "For this very reason
[because such promises are given to us], add to your
faith, virtue ; and to virtue, knowledge ; and to knowledge, temperance ; and to temperance, patience ; and
to patience, godliness ; and to godliness, brotherly kindness ; and to brotherly kindness, charity. For if these
things be in you, and abound, they make you that ye
shall neither be barren nor unfruitful in the knowledge
of our Lord Jesus Christ." The meaning is, not that
these things are to be the cause of fruitfulness, but that
they are fruitfulness itself. It is in these things that
fruitfulness consists. They shall *constitute* you "neither
barren nor unfruitful in the knowledge of our Lord."

Your mind already adverts to passages in which "the
fruit of the Spirit" is described. "The fruit of the
Spirit is love, joy, peace, long-suffering, gentleness, goodness, faith, meekness, temperance." "The fruit of the
Spirit is in all goodness, and righteousness, and truth."
Fruitfulness, as thus described, is the aim and appropriate result of those Divine influences by which the
soul is renewed in the likeness of God.

It is evident, then, what Christ means when he says
to his disciples, "Herein is my Father glorified, that ye
bear much fruit." Christian fruitfulness may be regarded as the effect of Divine truth received into a
believing mind, and incorporated into the soul's life.

It may be regarded as resulting from that spiritual
union between Christ and his disciples, which he
represents when he calls himself the vine, and them
the branches. It may be regarded as the true proficiency of a disciple in the knowledge of his Lord and
Saviour. It may be regarded as the fruit of that Holy
Spirit of promise by whom believers are sealed, and
who is the earnest of their inheritance. But under all
these aspects it is one and the same thing,—nothing
else than the maturity, the beauty, the worth, and the
blessedness of a complete Christian character.

I have already warned you, that a mistaken conception of what is meant by fruitfulness, may have the
effect of misdirecting your aspirations and endeavours
in the Christian life. Be careful, then, to set before
yourself a full and clear idea of what it is which constitutes productiveness and fruitfulness in the knowledge
of our Lord Jesus Christ. It is a too common error to
suppose that the fruitfulness of a Christian is to be
found, not simply in his own interior life, but rather in
results external to himself; not simply in what he
becomes under God's renewing and sanctifying work,
but rather in what he brings to pass, and in the conviction which he produces on other minds; not so much
in the reality of a life which is hid with Christ in God,
as in the outward manifestation and visibility of such a
life, in the impression which it makes on beholders, and
in the efficacy of its influence on the church or on the
world. If you take up such a notion of what you are

to aim at in undertaking and professing to follow Christ, you will be in danger of striving to *seem* holy instead of striving to *be* holy. You will be in danger of substituting the formalisms and conventionalisms that happen to be in vogue among the religious people of your acquaintance, for the simple reality of trusting in Christ and walking humbly with God. You will be in danger of falling into habits of religious affectation in manners and speech, and in demonstrations of sanctimony or of zeal, instead of simply striving to receive and obey the Word of Christ, to grasp the hope he sets before you, and to become like him in the temper and spirit of your mind. Instead of asking, in the simplicity of a believing and obedient spirit, what the God in whom you trust would have you do, and doing all things heartily as to the Lord and not to men, you will be continually and irresistibly tempted to ask, What will men say or think about me? how shall I make the right impression upon them? how shall I make them feel that my religion is a reality? All this tends to fix your mind more upon how you appear than upon what you are, and to make you more solicitous about the impressions and opinions of men than about what your own heart is in the sight of God. Thus it is that many a man falls by degrees into an unintended and unconscious hypocrisy; acquires a habit of using religious words and phrases by rote, and with little recollection or sense of what they mean; gradually assumes in his countenance and manner an expression which, being designed for impression, is unnatural, and perhaps repulsive. I do not warn you against seriousness and gravity of speech or of deportment, but this I say, watch and pray that you enter not into temptation ; watch and pray that you may *be* always under the full power of things unseen and eternal, rather than that you may *seem* so.

By the same sort of misconception you may be led to undervalue many of the most important elements of Christian character. It is easy for you to take up the notion that if only you can be what is called an active Christian, you will be of course a complete and eminent Christian. Sometimes we see a man who is conspicuous in efforts of one sort or another for the advancement of religion, zealous for the church, or for this or that religious enterprise, but who, in exercising himself unto godliness, is far from giving due attention to the things that are true and honest and just and lovely and of good report. It is easy for you to fall into just that error, and to assume that what Christ looks for in you is nothing else than zeal for the church, or zeal for the interest of religion. Do not think that I disparage religious activity as an element of Christian character, nor that I would in any way discourage or check your zeal to do all you can for Christ, and for the souls of men. On the contrary, I would have you understand distinctly, and remember, that the spirit of Christ in all his disciples is essentially a beneficent and active spirit, a spirit of zeal for God, and of aggression against the darkness and wickedness of this world. I would have you understand

M

that where there is no sympathy with Christ in his redeeming work, no compassion for those who are dead in
trespasses and sins, no love for the church and kingdom
of Christ, no readiness for self-denial in the service of
Christ, the spirit of Christ is not manifest.   There may
be an unblamed and unsuspected uprightness in all human
relations, and with it there may be combined a'most attractive personal amiableness like that of the young man
whom Jesus loved ; and yet, if there be no sympathy
with Christ and no readiness for self-sacrifice in his
service, the one thing lacking, as in the case of that
young man, implies a fatal deficiency.   But I would
have you understand also, and remember, that no manifestation of zeal for the Lord, no bustle or *éclat* of religious activity, no restlessness of endeavour in enterprises
of philanthropy, or of moral or religious propagandism,
no readiness to give, to suffer, or to die in behalf of a
principle, can turn the balance against the want of personal integrity, of strict veracity and honesty, of thorough
purity, of conscientiousness in all those ordinary and
homely virtues without which the profession of saintli-
ness is an abhorrence to God. A man may not only have
the gift of prophecy and understand all mysteries and all
knowledge without the principle of holy love ; he may
not only preach to others and be himself a castaway ;
he may even bestow all his goods to feed the poor, and
give his body to be burned, in the fervour of a zeal which
is not holy love and has no fellowship with Christ.   If
there be any virtue, if there be any praise, think on what-

soever things are true, whatsoever things are honest, whatsoever things are just, whatsoever things are pure, whatsoever things are lovely, whatsoever things are of good report. Remember that " the fruit of the Spirit is love, joy, peace, long-suffering, gentleness, goodness, faith, meekness, temperance." Remember that charity needs no conspicuousness of position, no celebrity or notoriety, no trophies of success, as essential to its reality. It suffereth long and is kind ; it envieth not ; it vaunteth not itself, is not puffed up, doth not behave itself unseemly, seeketh not its own, is not easily provoked, thinketh no evil, rejoiceth not in iniquity, but rejoiceth in the truth ; beareth all things, believeth all things, hopeth all things, endureth all things ; and in order to this it needs no splendour of gifts, no rare felicity of opportunities, no great cloud of mortal witnesses, no plaudits of this world's admiration. It may be as complete, as beautiful to the eye of God, and as true a manifestation of his glory, in the humblest position as anywhere else.

Some really conscientious persons, whose desire and purpose to follow Christ need not be doubted, seem to misunderstand, in part, the application of that precept : " Let your light so shine before men, that they may see your good works, and glorify your Father which is in heaven." Forgetful that it is the nature of light to shine, they do not observe that what the precept requires of them is simply that interior life of purity and love, that inward holiness which cannot but shine. If it be

said to the watchman on the mountain-top, "Let your
light shine," he has only to kindle his beacon, and its
warning flame flashes across the valleys. If it be said
to the keeper of a lighthouse, "Let your light shine,"
he has only to light up the lamp in his turret, and far
over the waves it shines. So when Christ says to us,
"Let your light shine before men,—let it so shine, that
they may see your good works, and glorify your Father
which is in heaven," we need not concern ourselves about
the impression which our conduct may make on other
minds; we need only take care that in thought, as well
as in word and deed, our lives are humble, holy, Christ-
like; and our light will shine, the self-same light that
shone in Christ. If we begin to be anxious about the
impression we are making upon men, we are immediately in danger of becoming like the hypocrites, whose
ruling motive in their works of outward goodness, or of
outward godliness, is that they may be seen of men. The
habit of doing things for effect or impression is dangerous. It is affectation; and affectation is, in its degree,
hypocrisy.

"Let this mind be in you, which was also in Christ."
It seems almost irreverent even to inquire what the effect
would be on our estimate of Christ's human character,
if we could imagine him as doing anything for the sake
of appearances. Who does not feel that the glory that
shines in the human life of our Redeemer would not be
there, but for his perfect unaffectedness? The glory of
Christ in his followers is dimmed, if it does not shine

naturally, and, as it were, unconsciously, " in simplicity and godly sincerity." So let your light shine.

Remember, then, that the aim of all your self-culture as a ·disciple of Christ must be, not the show and seeming of a Christian life, but the reality. A completely Christ-like character is to be valued for its own sake, and not for the sake of what men may think of it. God values it for what it is, and not for the impression which it makes. A truly and completely Christian character is nothing else than a Christ-like soul.

A Christ-like soul ! Think, you whose eye is on this page, how blessed it is to be like Christ, not in profession only, but in reality ; not only in the show and seeming of a Christian character, but in the soul's life. Think how possible it is for you to be thus blessed. Think of God's love to you, testified in Christ's self-sacrifice for you. Think of God's willingness to give the Holy Spirit to them that ask him. Think of those exceeding great and precious promises which are given to you in the gospel, that by them you may be a partaker of the Divine nature. It is possible for you to become—by God's mercy and gracious help, by his blessing on your diligence, by his answer to your prayers, by his performance of his promises—a Christ-like soul.

Is this your aspiration ? Are you hoping, praying, and striving to realize in your own experience the blessedness of a Christ-like soul ? There is no really Christian self-culture which aspires to anything less

than this.   Assuming that such is your aspiration, I
have endeavoured to help you by these friendly counsels, and to encourage you by showing that this is the
hope which the gospel sets before you.   All that I have
written is worthless to you, if you are not striving to
" put on the Lord Jesus Christ," and to be transformed
into his likeness " by the renewing of your mind."

Be assured that there is nothing extravagant or un-
warranted in your aspiring to all the dignity and blessedness of a Christ-like soul.   In truth, there is no other
just conception of a Christian life than this, that it is
the life of a renewed soul growing more and more like
Christ.   To " put on the new man" is nothing else than
to " put on Christ ;" and the new life is in us only
as that mind is in us which was also in Christ.   Ask
what the blessedness is to which they that love God
are " called according to his purpose."   Let an apostle
answer.   " Whom he did foreknow, he also did pre-
destinate "— to what ? — " to be conformed to the
image of his Son, that he might be the first-born among
many brethren" (Rom. viii. 28, 29).   It is to this that
you are invited.   " That ye might be partakers of the
divine nature," is the end for which are given all the
offers and promises which constitute the gospel.

If you have heartily undertaken the self-culture to
which the gospel calls us, you are already becoming a
Christ-like soul.   If you have received Christ, you are
of those whom he has made the sons of God,—himself the first-born among many brethren.   " Behold what

manner of love the Father hath bestowed on us, that we should be called the sons of God!" "It doth not yet appear what we shall be; but we know that, when he shall appear, we shall be like him, for we shall see him as he is." A Christ-like soul is a God-like soul; and that likeness to God, perfected in the soul, is the consummation of blessedness. Your assurance of hope is: "I shall be satisfied when I awake with thy likeness." Meanwhile, all the progress of your Christian self-culture is a progress in likeness to Christ, "whom not having seen ye love; in whom, though now ye see him not, yet believing, ye rejoice with joy unspeakable and full of glory, RECEIVING THE END OF YOUR FAITH, THE SALVATION OF YOUR SOULS."

EDINBURGH : T. CONSTABLE,
PRINTER TO THE QUEEN, AND TO THE UNIVERSITY.